# We and They

## Decolonizing Greco-Roman and Biblical Antiquities

# Aarhus Studies in Mediterranean Antiquity (ASMA)

## XIV

ASMA is a series of monographs and anthologies published by the research programme Classical Antiquity in the Department of Culture and Society, Aarhus University, Denmark. The programme includes researchers from a wide range of disciplines studying Graeco-Roman Antiquity, such as Classical Archaeology, Classical Philology, Ancient History, the Study of Religion, and Theology. The aim of the series is to publish significant new research in Classical Studies and to provide an interdisciplinary platform for the study of the ancient world. Thus, the series reflects both individual and collective scholarly engagements with new and innovative research of the highest international standard.

# We and They

## Decolonizing Greco-Roman and Biblical Antiquities

*Edited by*
*Jonathan Cahana-Blum*
*and Karmen MacKendrick*

Aarhus University Press |

We and They


Cover by: Jørgen Sparre
The book is typeset in Adobe Garamond and printed
by Narayana Press

ISBN 978 87 7184 443 6
ISSN 1399 2686

Aarhus University Press
Finlandsgade 29
DK-8200 Aarhus N
Denmark
www.unipress.dk

International distributors:
Oxbow Books Ltd.
The Old Music Hall
106-108 Cowley Road
Oxford, OX4 1JE
United Kingdom
www.oxbowbooks.com

ISD
70 Enterprise Drive, Suite 2
Bristol, CT 06010
USA
www.isdistribution.com

Published with the financial support of:
Aarhus University Research Foundation
Danish Council for Independant Research (Sapere Aude)

MIX
Papir fra ansvarlige kilder
FSC® C010651

PEER REVIEWED

/ In accordance with requirements of the Danish Ministry of Higher Education and Science, the certification means that a ph.d.-level peer has made a written assessment which justifies this book's scientific quality.

# Contents

# INTRODUCTION

In August 2016, 17 scholars from 9 countries and 3 continents gathered at Aarhus University Conference Center at Sandbjerg Estate, Denmark, to address a pertinent question: how do scholars address the we/they nexus when studying antiquity, and how does the frame of colonialism still function within this nexus, whether overtly or covertly? The conference abstract specifically noted those cases in which the difference between antiquity and modernity was stressed to the point where the scholar subsumed an ideal Western "we" and acted as an interpreter for the primitives of antiquity. During the conference itself, however, the participants demonstrated how such an approach is better understood on a spectrum, and underlined cases in which the people of antiquity have been co-opted into further modern political (and, ironically, often postcolonial) concerns. Thematically, the conference addressed issues of race and ethnicity, language and materiality, and gender and sexuality, to each of which a keynote was dedicated.

It has unfortunately proved impossible to include all the papers in this volume. Those included, however, provide a highly representative selection of both the problems and the solutions that were discussed during the lively three-day conference. These contributions also address different points on the we–they spectrum, and deal with each of the aforementioned themes.

The book opens with three highly methodological articles, two of which were given as keynotes in the conference. The first, by Manuela Giordano, addresses a classical text that has served as a paradigm for reading modern notions of race and ethnicity into antiquity. Aeschylus' *Persians* has been championed by Edward Said as the first representation of the Orient vis à vis the West. Giordano amply demonstrates that such an understanding is immersed in modern binary concepts, and that Aeschylus' text, far from confirming such a binary, is actually a haunting undermining of such dichotomies in an attempt to redefine Athenian identity as distinct from both Persian and (Greek) Homeric. Karmen MacKendrick's "Revelation at the Limit: Mystery and Matter after the Valentinians" engages with a different thrust in scholarship, in which antiquity is projected as the essential other of modernity. Reading Valentinian Gnosticism, which has been often considered "incomprehensibly distant from contemporary thought," MacKendrick demonstrates how a pertinent concept in this system, namely the Limit, can and should be brought into interesting and challenging conversation with modern concepts of materiality. The third introductory article, by Jonathan Cahana, takes up the ways in which a we/they dichotomy has hampered three otherwise sound analyses of ancient sexuality, and argues that effacing such a dichotomy would let us engage with the results of these analyses without the impeding baggage of colonial thought.

Each of the following articles engages with a case study under one of the major themes. Thus, Luca Pucci, Jessica van 't Westeinde, and Pieter van der Horst's essays all address issues of identity, race, and ethnicity. Pucci's analysis demonstrates how anthropological methods could be fruitfully applied in the historical study of ancient Greece through what he terms "constructive comparativism," so as to evade the "grounded statement that the modern European thought derives *recta via* from ancient Greece." Van 't Westeinde employs a thoroughly modern method – the cultural-evolutionary approach – in order to avoid a deeply entrenched modern inclination to dichotomize between Judaism and Christianity, an approach which, in turn, is itself enmeshed with the post-enlightenment understanding of "religion." Van der Horst's study addresses a sensitive and much avoided historical instance in which Jews were the perpetrators, rather than the victims, of religious persecution, and demonstrates how the study of Himyar social and political history has been hampered by relegating such cases to the impossible. No less sensitive is Makiko Sato's assessment of the way Augustine of Hippo reads the rape of Lucretia, and rape in general. By analyzing Augustine's concept of *sanctitas* and the way he applies it to the body and the soul, Sato questions whether Augustine can be subsumed under the frequently male perspective of victim-blaming, or instead offers victims a way to cope with the sexual violence they suffered, and still be considered pure within the patriarchal societies they inhabited. Concluding the volume is Anna Usacheva's article, which guides us through Origen's methods of textual criticism while underlining how our own understanding of the text – premised upon our printing press culture – could be highly misleading in evaluating Origen's approach.

All in all, the articles collected in this volume share a similar goal: to decolonize our understanding of antiquity, thus allowing modernity to converse with antiquity without constraining the latter to be either the direct precedent or the exact other of the former. It is certainly true that, as L.P. Hartley wrote in *The Go-Between*, the past is a foreign country. However, history has repeatedly demonstrated that colonialism never contributed to mutual understanding and constructive exchange of ideas – and that these are the dialogues we should strive for with our contemporaries, as well as with our ancestors.

# AESCHYLUS' PERSIANS

## Empathizing with the Enemy, or Orientalizing Them?

MANUELA GIORDANO

**ABSTRACT** *This article intends to put into perspective contemporary discourse on ethnic identity, and to analyse the oppositions us/them and friends/enemies in order to expose some hidden assumptions of the scholarly debate on the theme. In this sense, the fifth-century Athenian tragedy* Persians *by Aeschylus is a revealing case study, both for what it tells us regarding identity in ancient Greece and also as a lightning rod for modern projections of identity.*

Ethnic identity in the ancient Mediterranean entailed different levels and definitions of identity – ranging from a wider sense of belonging ('Greek', 'Roman', etc.) to a local, restricted one ('Athenian tribe') – articulating the interrelation of self and other in very different terms from the basic we/they opposition. Ethnic identity may be conveyed through multiple and diverse means, from political and military categories to ritual practices. As such, it may be defined as a dynamic construct that yields to processes of renegotiation and semantic remoulding over time.

Aeschylus' *Persians* was regarded by Edward Said as the first representation of the 'Orient' in Western culture, and many succeeding scholars have interpreted it as a way of defining Greek identity (=we) by representing the 'absolute otherness' of the Persians (=they). The following inquiry this interpretation as fundamentally grounded in a modern conception of a 'we' drastically opposed to a 'them', misleadingly applied to ancient Greek culture. Aeschylus' *Persians,* far from being an orientalist text, actually undermines that very basic tenet of the binary opposition we/they (positive/negative), and establishes identity in terms quite different from our etic categories.

Through an analysis of *Persians,* this article endeavours to reconstruct in emic terms a nuanced and multifaceted identitarian discourse of ancient Greek culture, made of diverse oppositions as well as of multiple similarities, a model which may prove unsettling for simplistic binary approaches to identity based on 'we' and 'they'.

***

## Hidden assumptions

We do not come to the subject of ethnic identity empty-handed but start, often inadvertently, with a stock of hidden assumptions and commonplaces that function as uncontroversial truths about our own categorizations of ethnic identity. In every field, commonplaces generate questions of their own, with an intrinsic structure of argumentation that almost inevitably leads us in a certain direction.

The first assumption is that the 'self' can be defined only in opposition to an 'other', which is often written with a capital letter, in a reification of this concept.[1] This is none other than the principle of non-contradiction, a pillar of Western logic, applied in our case to ethnic and national identity. As Aristotle put it, "the most certain of all principles" is that "it is impossible for the same attribute at the same time to belong and not to belong to the same thing and in the same relation" (Arist. *Metaph.* 4. 1005b. 19-20); in other words: "'A is B', and 'A is not B' are mutually exclusive." The principle of identity, developed thereafter, builds upon this, claiming that "each thing is the same as itself and different from another," or, "A is equal to A, and A is *not* B", where the negative conjunction should be highlighted. Applied to ethnic identity, as we interpret it today, it is only possible to define 'A', as in the case of an ethnic group or a nation-state, by opposing it to a 'B', that is, a 'they'. According to these principles, any identity is constructed by means of polarity and antithesis: Chechen–Russian, English–German, etc.

The second assumption is about the application of separative models and cosmologies to ancient cultures.[2] Our contemporary assumptions on ethnic identity are heavily influenced by our belonging to a nation-state. In a process that began in the nineteenth century and accelerated until the twentieth century, no part of the world was left unassigned or unlabelled, and ethnic feelings of belonging were slowly absorbed into national identities, a process that Benedict Anderson, among others, has masterfully retraced.[3] As a result, the vast majority of us were brought up with conceptions of boundaries and borders based on models of separation and mutually exclusive entities. Despite globalization as both an economic reality and a media discourse, we live in an epoch marked by the actual and ideal presence of borders and limits. It is not surprising that in scholarship, too, we risk projecting such separative models and cosmologies wherever our gaze lands, including onto ancient cultures.

If we view these assumptions from an historical perspective, however, we may easily discover that the idea of borders as precise lines clearly and cleanly separating two peoples or countries, however powerful, is very young in the history of human thought. There is nothing of its kind in the ancient world; even though modern national boundaries have become our exclusive "accessible parameters", to history, to use Archibald's phrase, they are "of little use when mapping the remote past, which blissfully ignores modern boundaries."[4]

### *Mediterranean assumptions*

Recently, more fitting paradigms and metaphors have been put forward to come to terms with these issues. Among them, the "network paradigm" seems particularly helpful, especially in its application to the Mediterranean area. This approach is much indebted to

1 See Browning 2002.

2 For the notion of 'separative cosmology' as opposed to 'interconnected cosmology', see Oudemans and Lardinois 1987.

3 Anderson 1991.

4 Archibald 2013, v. See also Giordano 2013.

Fernand Braudel, who was the first, and for a few decades the only, scholar to consider the Mediterranean in a new hermeneutic framework – that of the *nouvelle histoire*: viewing history from the perspective of a long duration (*longue durée*), thereby replacing the representation of history as unidimensional and linear.[5] This approach has been revived in the last two decades by Peregrine Horden, Nicolas Purcell and Irad Malkin, among others.[6] In their ambitious enterprise, Horden and Purcell have updated the Braudelian paradigm, reading Mediterranean history through the model of connectivity in a framework that allows unity and diversity to coexist, accounting for the fragmented and "fractalic" fabric of the Mediterranean, which is made up of micro-realities separated and independent, yet connected and united by the embedded connectivity of the sea.[7]

This Mediterranean paradigm of fluidity and connections allows us to recognize and analyze the model of separate national identities and histories, giving more scope to the traditional approach. The Mediterranean paradigm thus challenges "the 'origins' approach, according to which beginnings provide the meaning for what follows," as well as the idea of mutually exclusive ethnic identities, instead proposing "networks of exchange."[8] The world reconstructed by this approach stands out as polycentric; characterized by a substantial permeability, it is a world of interaction and "intimate cultural contacts," where ideas and cultural discoveries travelled along with people and goods.[9] To think in these "ancient" terms is to abandon the vision of a world separated into locked compartments – of modern nation-states with checkpoints and borders, passports and customs.[10] As Ian Morris has remarked, this paradigm is much indebted to the model of globalization, and as such is highly idealized.[11] In my opinion, however, we would do better not to stretch the parallel between the Mediterranean model and globalization too far. As I have hinted at above, globalization merely scratched the surface of the nation-state system. For our present purpose, it may be pointed out that the contemporary discourse on globalization has not deeply changed either the legal or the cultural perception of national and ethnic identities. While it often provides a rather ideological veneer of cosmopolitanism to serve hard economic, political, and financial facts, international regulations – including borders, legal status, and passport controls – are stricter than ever.[12]

---

5 Braudel 1966. See also Petropoulos 2006.

6 See Horden and Purcell 2000; Malkin 2005; Malkin, Constantakopoulou and Panagopoulou 2009.

7 On the metaphor of the "fractal" for the Mediterranean, see Malkin 2005a, 57.

8 See on this issue Abulafia 2003; for an integration of this paradigm with Greek history see Malkin 2005, 2; Malkin 2009; Morris 2005.

9 Burkert 1992, 21.

10 See Stoddart and Cifani 2012; McInerney 2014 for the issue of identity in the Mediterranean framework.

11 Morris 2005, part. 50-51.

12 As Ross Douthat 2016 has remarked, "People who consider themselves 'cosmopolitan' in today's West, by contrast, are part of a meritocratic order that transforms difference into similarity, by plucking the best and brightest from everywhere and homogenizing them into the peculiar species

Consistently and contrary to modern national identities, throughout antiquity or at least late antiquity, ethnic identity envisaged different levels and definitions of identity, ranging from a wider sense of belonging ('Greek', 'Roman', etc.) to a local, restricted one ('Athenian tribe').

Rather than a self-perception based on duality, a multiple self-perception remained the dominant model of ethnic identity: "the rule rather than the exception."[13] That the ancient notion of ethnicity is both slippery and multi-layered has become a commonly held assumption.[14] Famous examples of this include Philip II of Macedonia, who was considered both a barbarian and a Greek, and whose ancestry was traced back to Heracles (Demosth. 3. 26; 18, 68), a "Barbarian from Pella."[15] Another paradigmatic figure is Paul of Tarsus, a citizen of a Cilician city, an authoritative member of a Jewish community, a Roman citizen, and a leader of Christian communities across the Roman Empire.

Such a variety of modes of ethnic belonging articulates the interrelation of self and other in very different terms from the basic we/they opposition, which is "intolerant of divided loyalties or grey areas."[16]

## Ancient Greece

If in such a world the principle of identity that opposes one people to another is of little use, ancient Greece was no exception. However much we like to draw our modern identity from ancient Greek realities, we would do better to avoid any 'either/or' rationale and try to articulate our assumptions as much as possible. As Archibald has recently phrased it, "there was no such a thing as a 'contact zone' between two compartmentalized worlds, the 'civilized' world and the 'barbarian' world, only many networks of exchange, commercial, cultural and intellectual. The idea of a cultural divide may have existed at an abstract level, but it did not exist in spatial terms."[17]

Having said this, in a famous passage, Herodotus defines *to hellēnikon*, 'Greekness', or 'the Greek thing', as follows (Hdt 8. 144. 2):

> τὸ Ἑλληνικὸν ἐὸν ὅμαιμόν τε καὶ ὁμόγλωσσον καὶ θεῶν ἱδρύματάνά τε κοινά καὶ θυσίαι ἤθεά τε ὁμότροπα
>
> Greekness consists in having the same blood, the same language, and common shrines of the gods and sacrifices, as well as a similar way of life.

---

that we call 'global citizens'... Their vision of history's arc bending inexorably away from tribe and creed and nation-state looks to outsiders like something familiar from eras past: a powerful caste's self-serving explanation for why it alone deserves to rule the world."

13 Browning 2002, 258.

14 On ethnic identity in ancient Greece, see Cartledge 1993, 36-62; Hall 1997; Luce 2007; Hall 2009; Hornblower 2008; Gruen 2011; Stoddart and Cifani 2012.

15 Isocr., Philip. 32; for Argos as his fatherland, see Isocr. Panegir. 50.

16 Browning 2002, 257.

17 Archibald 2013, 127.

These words give us important pointers in terms of a common language, cults and kinship, that is, common descent, whether real or imagined. As we will see, however, it would be hasty and misleading to say that those who did not share these characteristics were for the Greeks an 'other', or 'they'.

Ancient Greece was communalistic and polis-oriented, and the source of social life was the polis to which one belonged, where the human group was foremost: Athens is not "the city of Athens" but "the city of the Athenians," that is, it is the human, social group that gives existence to the city in an interactive relationship between the individual and the community. The territory is given meaning by virtue of its relationship with the community. In the shaping of this communal identity the role of civic gods has a fundamental symbolic function. The civic gods, although they share many features with the Panhellenic elements, represent the city itself as linked to a particular territory and distinct from any other polis.

If by and large the Greeks defined themselves in terms of their belonging to a polis, that is, to an independent political unity, they also felt a strong belonging to an *ethnos* – a wider group with territorial or linguistic affinity.[18] In both cases, the language of ethnic belonging is that of kinship. Typically, feeling part of the same group, whether small or large, invariably means having a common ancestor; as Hall has it: "Above all else, though, it must be the myth of shared descent which ranks paramount among the features that distinguish ethnic from other social groups."[19] But common ancestry was not used to make sharp distinctions between people; in fact, common ancestry was often created for the purpose of forming a temporary alliance and, as has been shown by Robin Osborne, was a very flexible, *ad hoc* tool of identity fabrication.[20] Osborne has deconstructed the centrality of ethnic identity in political life and abruptly asserted that in ancient Greece, "Ethnicity plays a part that is at best secondary and in most cases completely negligible."[21]

It is extremely revealing that, for the Athenians, foreign affairs considered relationships with other Greek *poleis* at the same level as those with other non-Greek societies, kingdoms and the like. In fact, beyond the limits of the community, everyone was a *xeinos*, a stranger and a potential guest-friend. The very word *xeinos* reveals the ambiguity of the notion of the stranger, because it means both 'enemy' and 'guest'. The stranger to the community can be a potential enemy, but a potential partner too.[22] Non-Greek-speaking Mediterranean neighbours were not regarded as absolutely 'other', or at least no more than Greek-speaking members of another polis. The practice of Greek colonization clearly demonstrates how ancient Greeks approached neighbouring traditions: settlers, upon arriving on foreign territory to found a colony, brought with them the sacred flame taken from the hearth of the motherland and its cults, but also

18 Osborne 2012, 24.

19 Hall 1997, 25, see also 40–51.

20 Osborne 2012.

21 Osborne 2012, 30.

22 On the complexities of *xenia* see Herman 1987.

offered sacrifices to local gods as a prerequisite for the rites of foundation. This is an example of the appropriation of other cultures through transformation and translation into Greek categories, a phenomenon that highlights a double attitude of openness and appropriation, rather than one of separation and domination.[23] Not only did ancient Greek models envisage different levels of ethnic or group belonging, but they did so through an encompassing and non-exclusive model of identity.

## Aeschylus' *Persians*: a case study

A central piece of evidence for the current debate about ethnicity and the "invention of the barbarian" is the fifth-century Athenian tragedy *Persians* by Aeschylus. In the following I will reconstruct in emic terms the nuanced and multifaceted identitarian discourse of ancient Athenian culture as observed at a specific time, 472 BCE, in a specific place, Athens, and by a specific speaker, the playwright Aeschylus.

This tragedy has a twofold relevance: not only does it explicitly stage the conflict between the Greeks and the 'barbarian' Persians, which became the archetypal victory of Western freedom over Oriental slavery in the imagination of much later Western discourse,[24] but it was also regarded by Edward W. Said as the first representation of the 'Orient' in Western culture, a sort of blueprint for the conceptualization of the East, represented by the Persians, and the West, represented by the ancient Greeks. In Aeschylus' *Persians*, Said asserts, "Asia speaks through and by virtue of the European imagination, which is depicted as victorious over Asia, that hostile 'other' world beyond the sea."[25]

In Said's wake, many scholars have interpreted the play as defining Greek identity (=we) by 'othering' the Persians (=they). Among them, Edith Hall, in her influential *Inventing the Barbarian*, writes:

"The tragedy is not ornamented in oriental colouring, but suffused with it, it represents the first unmistakable file in the archive of Orientalism, the discourse by which European imagination has dominated Asia ever since by conceptualizing its inhabitants as defeated, luxurious, emotional, cruel and always as dangerous. The language in which the *Persae* expresses its Orientalism is a daring result of the poet's search … for a new literary language in which to imply the ascendency of Hellas and express the 'otherness' of the invader."[26]

Before tackling the 'othering' thesis, let us first have a general look at Aeschylus' *Persians*. The tragedy revolves around the battle of Salamis, the decisive event of the Persian wars, where the Greek fleet and army, led by the Athenians, unexpectedly and despite their small numbers, crushed the Persian fleet at the small island of Salamis, near Athens, in 480 BCE. The tragedy is set in the Persian royal court, and stars Queen Atossa, the mother of King Xerxes, and his faithful counsellors. The news of the battle

23 See Malkin 1998.

24 See Rhodes, Hall, MacIntosh 2008.

25 Said 1978, 56.

26 Hall 1989, 99-100.

is reported by a Persian messenger, and the tragedy represents the mournful reaction of the Persians to the news, eventually staging the ghost of Darius and the arrival of Xerxes, dressed in rags.[27] It is important to stress that the whole event is narrated and represented through the eyes of the Persian enemy, whose feelings of bereavement are presented with great emphasis. The historical conjuncture is no less meaningful: the play was staged in 472, only eight years after the battle of Salamis. In 476 the playwright Phrynicus in his *Phoenician Women* exalted Athens and her naval power through the enemy's point of view, and the playwright's sponsor, the *choregos*, was the very proponent and champion of that same naval prowess and power, Themistocles. Four years later, Aeschylus represented the same event, reprising Phrynicus, indirectly quoted at the beginning of the tragedy, and likewise representing the battle through the enemy's account; the sponsor was none other than a young Pericles.

The historical context of the tragedy is marked by the emergence of Athens as a martial power. After the battle of Salamis, Athenians experienced a rapid increase in both military and cultural prestige, culminating in 477 with the foundation of the Delian League. This inaugurated a singular period: all the League's campaigns were victorious until 465. At a short distance from the extraordinary successes of the 490s and 480s, from Marathon to Mycale, Athenians were continuously ready to fight, unerringly engaged in military campaigns at the risk of their lives, earning victory after victory. It is important to stress that these military undertakings and the glorious days they brought to Athens had an enormous impact in terms of identity.[28] "Where on the earth do they say that Athens is? "Asks queen Atossa at line 231 of Aeschylus' *Persians*.[29] Unlike other Greek *poleis* – Thebes, Corinth, Argos, and even Sparta – Athens was not even on the map of heroic Greece: the Athenians were remarkable for their absence from the great Panhellenic feat, the Trojan war, and could certainly not claim a primary role in the hitherto established Panhellenic heroic past. In the years of the *Persians*, the Athenians were therefore in need of a tradition that could legitimate their power by projecting back into the past the greatness of their present, that is, a narration able to represent the Athens of the present time as heroic and in continuity with the actual past. A new, martial Athenian identity required narratives and myths bearing the marks of novelty and antiquity simultaneously. Such stories would recognize Athens' change in standing by providing a lineage narrative that could also serve – and increasingly so – to assert afresh their position in the Delian league. *Persians* responds to this need for new tales and myths that would (re)invent an Athenian tradition.

This historical context helps us to understand the value and meaning of the battle of Salamis for the Athenians. In tracing the new lines of their identity, the confrontation with the Persians was instrumental in defining Greek and Athenian identities.

27 See Garvie 2009.

28 See Giordano 2016.

29 See Hall 1996, 127; Harrison 2000, 140, n. 9.

*Persians vs Athenians?*

This drama presents possibly the first recorded self-presentation of the Athenians. The rapid exchange between Atossa and the Chorus, immediately before the messenger reports the disaster of Salamis, is perhaps the most insightful and explicit in this regard, since the Chorus gives an answer to the question "who are the Athenians and what are they like?" (231-245):

| | |
|---|---|
| **Ἄτοσσα**<br>ὦ φίλοι, ποῦ τάς Ἀθήνας φασὶν ἱδρῦσθαι χθονός. | **Atossa**<br>Meanwhile, my friends, I would like to learn where Athens is located. |
| **Χορός**<br>τῆλε πρὸς δυσμαῖς ἄνακτος Ἡλίου φθινασμάτων. | **Chorus**<br>Far from here, to the west where the last rays of our Lord the Sun set. |
| **Ἄτοσσα**<br>ἀλλά μὴν ἵμειρ᾽ ἐμὸς παῖς τήνδε θηρᾶσαι πόλιν; | **Atossa**<br>Can it then really be that my son had the keen desire to make this city his prey? |
| **Χορός**<br>πᾶσα γάρ γένοιτ᾽ ἂν Ἑλλς βασιλέως ὑπήκοος. | **Chorus**<br>Yes, for then all Hellas would be subject to the King. |
| **Ἄτοσσα**<br>ὧδέ τις πάρεστιν αὐτοῖς ἀνδροπλήθεια στρατοῦ; | **Atossa**<br>Does their army have such a multitude of men? |
| **Χορός**<br>καὶ στρατὸς τοιοῦτος, ἔρξας πολά δὴ Μήδους κακά. | **Chorus**<br>Yes, it is an army of such magnitude that it has caused great disaster for the Medes. |
| **Ἄτοσσα**<br>καὶ τί πρὸς τούτοισιν ἄλλο; πλοῦτος ἐξαρκὴς δόμοις; | **Atossa**<br>And what else have they besides? Do they have sufficient wealth in their homes? |
| **Χορός**<br>ἀργύρου πηγή τις αὐτοῖς ἐστι, θησαυρὸς χθονός. | **Chorus**<br>Of silver they possess a veritable fountain, a treasure chest in their soil. |
| **Ἄτοσσα**<br>πότερα γρ τοξουλκὸς αἰχμὴ δι χεροῖν αὐτοῖς πρέπει; | **Atossa**<br>Is the bow-stretching arrow particularly suited to their hands? |

| Χορός<br>οὐδαμῶς: ἔγχη σταδαῖα καὶ φεράσπιδες σαγαί. | **Chorus**<br>Far from it; they have lances for close fight and shields that serve them for armor. |
|---|---|
| Ἄτοσσα<br>τίς δὲ ποιμάνωρ ἔπεστι κἀπιδεσπόζει στρατῷ; | **Atossa**<br>And who is set over them as shepherd and is master of their host? |
| Χορός<br>οὔτινος δοῦλοι κέκληνται φωτὸς οὐδ᾽ ὑπήκοοι. | **Chorus**<br>Of no man are they called the slaves or vassals. |
| Ἄτοσσα<br>πῶς ἂν οὖν μένοιεν ἄνδρας πολεμίους ἐπήλυδας; | **Atossa**<br>How then can they withstand the attack of an invading foe? |
| Χορός<br>ὥστε Δαρείου πολὺν καὶ καλὸν φθεῖραι στρατόν | **Chorus**<br>So well as to have destroyed Darius' great and courageous host |

This passage artfully combines two perspectives, which we may venture to define as etic and emic, where Atossa represents the former and the Chorus the latter. In inquiring about the Athenians, the Persian queen makes use of the values, parameters and models of Persian culture (or of Persian culture as seen through the Athenian etic perspective), according to which an enemy may be defined as strong, fearsome and powerful. These are: 1) numbers – the size of their army; 2) wealth – the amount of treasure that the people store; and 3) their skill in archery. By Persian standards the Athenians seem entirely deficient, without a single distinctive feature that would constitute a mighty opponent. And yet, by way of opposition, Aeschylus draws a powerful image of the Athenians: frugal and modest, few yet unswerving, free, peer-ranked, masters of themselves, anonymous and steadfast close-fighters. In so doing, he presents the Athenians with their newly forged skills: ability in risk-taking, keeping quiet and staying put even when overcome by mad fear of a great enemy, and cohesiveness to the point that the division between self and the group dissolves. This is what, possibly for the first time, *Persians* showed (off), subtly and yet powerfully – implicitly, and yet recognizably. Aeschylus' intention as a poet was not merely aesthetic: he played a central role in constructing a public discourse for martial purposes. By showing them what they had developed and judging their martial abilities, he primed the citizen warrior body to act in the same way in their yearly undertakings against the Persians. The opposition to the Persians is certainly functional for the creation of the Athenians' self-representation, but it would be rash to think that this involves a clear-cut opposition between the Persian Asian Orient (= Them) and Athenian Greek West (= We) in terms of bad and good, and that, in the words of Said, "Asia speaks through and by virtue of the European imagination, which is depicted as victorious over Asia, that hostile 'other' world beyond the sea."[30] As the following will show, Aeschylus was indeed setting up an opposition, but one that complicates, and perhaps shockingly so, any East/West, We/They opposition.

### *Homeric Persians*

Are the Persians really just Persians? I do not think so. Size, riches, and a massive, multi-ethnic (flock-like) army, obedient and subservient under the supreme command of the king-shepherd, are the markers of another, perhaps even too familiar, mighty host: the Greek army of the *Iliad*. The description of the Persian side is thoroughly clothed in Homeric language, values, and material. This fact, to the best of my knowledge, has gone quite unnoticed, and it acquires a crucial relevance in our investigation. It would be both misleading and reductive to speak of a mere 'literary device': these are not harmless Homeric 'usages'. The Homeric presentation of the Persians is pivotal to the Athenian emancipation from the Panhellenic past as told by Homeric narrative, and responds to the need to found a new Athenian tradition even greater than the epic one. Until that point, to speak of the past was to speak of Homer and epics,[31] and in order for the Athenians to reconsider themselves and their relationship to the Panhellenic context, it was necessary to revisit and reframe the Homeric paradigm itself. Typical constituents of Homeric warfare scenes and characters thus undergo a process, more or less implicit, of opposition, reversal, displacement, and estrangement, with the effect of projecting a Homeric double, as a shade, onto the Persians. What stands as a marker of excellence in the Homeric context takes on an obviously negative character in *Persians*. The banners of prestige in Homer – gold and riches, and a great, obedient, sheep-like army – in Aeschylus are reversed and portend disaster, dangerous excess, and intrinsically vulnerable passivity. The Persian court and army flow with riches, just like Agamemnon's Mycene, against which Athenian houses appear modest. The Persians are ruled by a shepherd-king, in keeping with Homeric style; Agamemnon and the king in general is a *poimen laon* (ποιμὴν λαῶν), that is, the symbol of the 'rule of one'. On the other hand, the Athenians herald a new and different conception of *kratos*: the 'rule of all', embodied in an army of peer-ranked citizens, empowered by their individual responsibility and agency, a far cry from the Homeric (and Persian) sheep-like army.[32] If the Persians are represented as tyrannical, luxurious, and excessive, the brunt of the opposition strikes much closer to the Homeric-aristocratic type of warrior than to the Persian as 'Asiatic other'.

The 'othering' process at work seems therefore to be between the hallowed Homeric Greek model and the present Athenian one. From this perspective, it is difficult to endorse the thesis of Aeschylus "orientalizing" the Persian enemy, so that "the tragedy is not ornamented in oriental colouring, but suffused with it." Rather, the tragedy is suffused with a Homeric colouring, which proves instrumental to a different kind of

30 Said 1978, 56.

31 Easterling 1997, 25, 53.

32 See Cartledge 2009.

opposition: Aeschylus is somehow 'persianizing' the Homeric narratives and heroes, thus distancing them from the Athenian present.

*Persian kinship*

At lines 181-187, Atossa recounts to the Chorus a disquieting dream she had the previous night:

> I dreamed that two women in beautiful clothes, one in Persian garb, the other in Dorian attire, appeared before my eyes; both far more striking in stature than are the women of our time, flawless in beauty, sisters of the same family (κασιγνήτα γένους ταὐτοῦ). As for the lands in which they dwelt, to one had been assigned by lot the land of Hellas, to the other that of the barbarians.

There we are: Asia and Greece, the Orient and the West, to use the Saidian dichotomy, whose division Aeschylus is supposed to have constructed for the first time in the *Persians*. Yet they are not two opposed strangers, but "two sisters of the self-same blood" (l. 185-186), the self-same lineage, *genos*. Not only do they meet the common Greek criterion of ethnic identity according to Herodotus mentioned above (having a common ancestor), but they do so in a an extreme way – coming from the same parents, the same womb. However 'other' the Persian barbarians may seem from the Greek point of view, they are, following Aeschylus' metaphor, estranged siblings.

In many parts of the play, moreover, the Persians are in fact very Greek as far as cultural assumptions are concerned. When speaking of Persian cities, for example, they speak of a *polis*, the very foundation of all Greek civic identity. After the dream of Atossa, the chorus suggests she offer a sacrifice and a prayer to the gods, wishing favorable things "for you, your children, for the city (*polei*) and all the friends."[33]

Throughout the play we see a process of assimilation at work, which collapses the very dichotomy of we/they as we conceive it, of 'self' and 'non-self'. As to Hall's thesis, Bakewell asks "what are the implications for her thesis if Aeschylus encodes the Persians as 'other' at one moment and (at least partially) as 'self' (i.e., Greek) the next?"[34]

*Empathizing with the enemy?*

The last point I wish to raise is one of perspective: what are we to make of the fact that events are recounted from the enemy's point of view? Writing between the two World Wars, the Hellenist Gilbert Murray considered that the equanimous attitude expressed by Aeschylus towards the Persian enemy should have been held as a model by the Brit-

33 See also l. 213, and 556, politais.

34 Bakewell 1997. He further notes: "Is there not a third component to the portrait, whereby Aeschylus, wittingly or not, encodes the great enemy not so much 'other' as 'self'? If this is so, where do the differences between Persian and Greek give way to similarities? And what are the implications for our reading of the play? It seems incumbent on Hall to address systematically instances where the Persians appear to operate within 'Greek' frames of reference."

ish towards the Germans.[35] In a similar vein, Simon Goldhill remarks that the very fact of staging a *kommos* (a dirge) for the Persian enemy in a public setting such as the Dionysia is an extraordinary thing, and "If sympathy for others is part of the 'tragic experience', it is none the less part of what I see as Aeschylus' boldness in this play to place an audience in the position of discovering tragic sympathy for such an 'other' as the Persian invaders."[36] I agree that there is much creative boldness in Aeschylus' staging of lamentation; still, as we will see, the "tragic sympathy" Athenians discovered for the Persian invaders cannot possibly have been wholehearted. At the very opposite extreme, as we have seen, is Hall's position; following Said, she considers the *Persians* the first instance of Orientalism. As Thomas Harrison has remarked, the freedom from xenophobia and humility in victory is a modern projection, but it does not necessarily follow, as Harrison has it, that the play is fundamentally unsympathetic towards the enemy.[37] If a xenophobic, orientalizing interpretation does not seem appropriate to understanding the *Persians*, how far can we go in speaking about compassion, or even empathy with the enemy? Does the focus on the Persians' hopes, fears, and sufferings "compel compassion for the vanquished," as Peter Burian asserts?[38]

Neither interpretation seems fully adequate. In 472, the Persians were the Athenians' sworn enemies, and Athens had risked utter destruction and slavery at their hands only a few years before, prompting the formation in 477 of the Delian League to pursue the fight against the Persians.[39] And yet, would they have wanted them all dead and gone? Were the Persians the utterly 'Oriental other', an inhuman foil for the Athenians, to be scorned and despised? The answer is: not quite. Not only does Aeschylus show a remarkable respect towards the Persians and their grief, but the extent of Persian–Greek interaction in the fifth century is becoming clearer all the time, ever since Miller showed that Persian culture entered Athenian life in multifarious ways in this period; our approach to Persian–Greek relations has consequently become much more nuanced and articulated.[40] While Aeschylus was staging his *Persians*, therefore, the interaction between Greeks and Persians was "intense and multi-faceted"; hostility coexisted with an exchange "able to prevail, largely unaffected by geo-political friction."[41]

Should this lead us to conclude that Aeschylus showed in his play the value of equanimity and impartiality towards the enemy? Again: not quite.

We can surmise that the Athenians occasionally did hate the Persians, but at the same time they were capable of identifying with their suffering as represented on stage, however admittedly various the reactions to such a dramatization might have been. We know for sure that they were tremendously attracted to them. Despite the principle of

---

35 Murray 1940, 127-128.

36 Goldhill 1988, 193 n. 35.

37 Harrison 2000, 193.

38 Burian 1997, 186.

39 See also Rosenbloom 1993.

40 Miller 1997; Raaflaub 2009 with bibliography.

41 Rollinger 2006, 212.

contradiction, they perceived the Persians as both 'other' and 'self'. They admired them and scorned them, swore to pursue them until they fled far from the Greek world, but also deftly copied their ways.[42]

It is equally important to remind ourselves that the recognition of common human suffering was a customary way of thinking in ancient Greece, and that two archenemies may show a paradoxical compassion towards each other. Book 24 of the *Iliad* illustrates this powerfully: it portrays the old Trojan king Priam kneeling in front of Achilles, kissing the hands that had cruelly slain Hector, Priam's beloved heir. The old king supplicates the young hero to ransom the body of his son (*Il.* 24. 507-512): "'and in Achilles he roused desire to weep for his father; and he took the old man by the hand, and gently put him from him. So the twain bethought them of their dead, and wept; the one for man-slaying Hector wept sore, [510] the while he grovelled at Achilles' feet, but Achilles wept for his own father, and now again for Patroclus; and the sound of their moaning went up through the house."[43] The scene of the two enemies crying together, each for his own dead, shows the sharing of such emotions and a recognition of the 'other' as 'self'.

## Conclusions

It is in an ultimately constructive frame of mind that I have challenged a famous interpretation of the *Persians* as fundamentally grounded in a modern conception of a 'we' drastically opposed to a 'they'. In particular, I have highlighted Aeschylus' decision to represent the Persians through Homeric references in the use of epic style, characters, and values.[44] This reveals itself to be a doubly significant discursive practice: on the one hand, Aeschylus presents the Persians with the majestic and magnificent identity of the Homeric Panhellenic heroes, while on the other, this allusion estranges the Homeric model as far as it is associated with the enemy. As a result, the Athenian playwright redefines Athenian identity in new and finer terms, creating a distance from both Homer and the Persian, whose identities are remote and familiar at the same time, and cannot be reduced to a simple opposition. If Aeschylus' *Persians* undermines that very basic tenet of the binary opposition we/they as positive/negative, it does so to establish the category of 'identity' in very different terms, forcing us to question our own etic categories.

In conclusion, in order to understand ancient ideas of ethnic identity, we must question the foundations of our notions and acknowledge the fact that commonplaces, unbeknownst to us, work in shaping our perceptions and discourse, in this case, of ethnic identity.

If we go back to the hidden assumptions of contemporary discourses on identity, we may wonder who is really seeing 'oriental suffusion' on the Persian side, Aeschylus

42 See also Archibald 2013, 124, who speaks of the "mixed emotions triggered by the phenomenon of Persian occupation" of the area of the north Aegean.

43 Translated by Murray 1924.

44 On the notion of 'representation' in this sense see Said 1976, 20-22. I will deal more thoroughly elsewhere with the militant critique of Aeschylean tragedy vis à vis Homer.

or us. This may serve as a warning – this changing 'other' may be more in the mind of modern critics who, in the attempt to be politically correct and sensitive in terms of postcolonial Saidian thinking, end up forcing onto the ancient texts those very same categories they are trying to detect and dispel, but that ultimately rest in our own worldview and commonplaces: West and Orient, self and other, we and they.[45]

45 For further textual argumentation, see Giordano forthcoming.

# REVELATION AT THE LIMIT

## Mystery and Matter after the Valentinians

**ABSTRACT** *In both popular and scholarly perspectives, the religious ideas and practices labeled Gnostic are widely considered to be almost incomprehensibly distant from contemporary thought, both because of their deliberate mystery and because they are so insistently theological. This essay argues that at least one important Gnostic concept, the idea of Limit in Valentinianism, can actually take its place in and make interesting contributions to contemporary philosophical debates about materiality.*

The reputation of Gnostic practice and doctrine is that of something covert – hidden, suppressed, possibly dangerous. Hollywood films and popular literature suggest that some version of Gnosticism is the long-repressed other of Christianity, a shocking truth that could destroy the Catholic Church in particular, a beautiful egalitarianism that threatens the ecclesial hierarchy. A somewhat more knowledgeable tradition reads Gnosticism, broadly construed, as the other *within* Christianity, officially denied but responsible for most of the detrimental elements of the latter.[1] As one might expect, the actual history is more complex. Christian Gnostic sects do become officially heretical in Christianity, but they did not begin as distinct rejections of an established orthodoxy, nor are they without lasting influence. In this essay, I would like to return to one particular aspect of thought in one particular Gnostic mode – specifically, to the role of Limit in Valentinian thought – which has *not* had a clear enduring influence.[2] However, the theories of existence and knowledge that we find there turn out to have some intriguing intersections with the humanities' recent returns to materialism. I should warn the reader now that in order to make these comparisons, I offer a rather offbeat reading of the Valentinian mythos, and only a few salient points and positions from some very diverse and contentious present-day traditions. In the references here,

1 One seminal figure in this line of thought is Eric Voegelin, whose criticisms rest on the realized eschatology of many Gnostic groups – the claim that redemption is not only to be found in an otherworldly afterlife. He saw this tendency in many political as well as theological attempts at reform. The most relevant works are collected in Voegelin 1999. For the nearly opposing criticism that Gnosticisms are hostile to the world that God has made, we can go all the way back to Irenaeus 1992, 1.21.3, where he describes a baptismal ceremony that includes the words "I redeem my soul from this world and from all things derived from it." For a summary of other relevant texts, see Brons, undated c.

2 Valentinian doctrine comes very close to Christian orthodoxy in many ways, so that some people who accept the term Gnostic nonetheless would not include Valentinianism there. Fortunately, this open debate is not germane to my argument here.

however, there will be resources for further exploration, should anyone be drawn (as I always am) by the complications.

It is a theological commonplace to say that human comprehension of divine things is limited, but few have done as much with the idea of limit as the Valentinians, who flourished from the second to the fourth centuries of the common era. In their cosmology (that is, their theory of how the world comes to be), Limit acts as a restriction, but a creative one. In their soteriology (their theory of salvation), Limit acts as a revelation, and a salvific one. An understanding of these multiple roles of Limit requires a detour through Plato, from which we shall finally emerge into a rather fascinating entanglement of reality, knowledge, and desire, one that offers both a complication of and an alternative to some recent philosophical proposals and positions.

## Cosmology

Valentinian cosmology begins with a One, "the inconceivable uncontained," as the Gospel of Truth repeatedly says. And it adds, "The entirety was inside of him – the inconceivable uncontained, who is superior to all thought."[3] If the All (a more common translation of entirety) are inside the One, how do they ever become anything that is not the One? This is where Limit comes in. The One thinks itself, and brings forth Limit. In the Valentinian Exposition, we read, "And the Boundary... [separated] the All...... ...is totally ineffable to the All, and the confirmation and actualization of the All."[4] (The term *Horos* is sometimes translated into English as *limit*, other times as *boundary*. I have used *limit* in my own text but kept to the translations I have used when quoting.) There are many components of the All (they are called Aeons), but they all have their root in the One, and are made other than One by Limit. Limit is what allows any one thing to *be*, apart from another.

In other words, that creation might be, the One (also called the Father) establishes Limit within itself, by some mode of thought (we shall have to inquire later about that mode).[5] Across the Limit is every state of being, every thing, that is not One. It is by Limit that *any*thing is, that *all* things are. What makes this even more strange is that according to Irenaeus, who carefully chronicled Valentinian and other "heresies," the Father emitted the Limit in his own image, without another, "as part of no conjugal couple."[6] So the Limit, which seems to keep other things apart from the One, is the image of the One, which cannot have parts or divisions. The Limit is in the image of the illimitable. Whatever knowledge this gives us, of whatever complex cosmos, is going to have to be something other than comprehension.

In the realm of the All, the Aeons are paired, masculine and feminine. These pairings are reflective of the androgyny of the divine. Despite the name "Father," the One is

3 Layton 1987b, 17.5-6.

4 Thomassen and Meyer 2007, 25. Ellipses original.

5 Brons undated d also notes Irenaeus 1992, 1.2.1, and Thomassen and Meyer 2007, 27.36-37.

6 Irenaeus 1992, 1.2.4.

neither male nor female, or both male and female; the paired Aeons are not so much reinforcements of heterosexual bonding as they are aspects of a One beyond binaries. As one might expect, there are many variations and details regarding the layers and the sequence of this creation. To maintain clarity, I will not detail these here; they most often have to do with the order, the names, and the exact number of emanations, and do not directly affect the description of Limit.[7]

As the One is designated Father, the Limit is called the Son. Only the Son knows the Father, because there is nothing between them (if there were, what came between would be another limit, another edge or boundary).[8] The Limit keeps the Aeons from knowing the Father completely. Only by this can their existence be sustained, as otherwise they would be absorbed into Oneness. One of the Aeons is Sophia, wisdom. She thinks that she can know the father through thinking alone, and she tries to do so, without the aid of her consort, who is variously called the ordained, the longed-for, or the perfect. Not only does she not succeed in her pursuit of knowledge; in punishment for her rejection of limitation she is excluded from the All by another, narrower limit, and she and her consort are separated.[9] This punishment, of course, also protects her from absorption.

This distresses her. She weeps, and the other Aeons join in her pleas for help and for mercy.[10] Limit comes to the rescue, dividing her into higher and lower Sophias. Higher Sophia is re-included in the all, and returns to her consort.[11] Once more she is part of a pair, an image of completeness. Lower Sophia, however, continues to suffer. Her suffering generates materiality. But she too receives assistance, first in the form of memory. When she remembers the goodness where she once was, she repents of her actions, and her repentance gives rise to soul.[12] Then the Son, the Limit, now in its role as savior, descends into materiality to free her from sadness.[13] Thus saved, she gives birth to spirit. The seeds of the spirit are within material beings, however, and not in some alternate realm. Matter from sorrow, soul from repentance, and spirit from recollected joy are all in the world.

It sounds as if matter is bad, the product of suffering, cut away twice from the divine source of all that is. It turns out, though, that the Valentinian attitude toward matter

---

7 See especially Thomassen and Meyer 2007, 29.25-37. Glossed in Brons undated d.

8 For a list of the sources for these variations, see Brons undated d.

9 There is another version of Valentinian cosmology, which is closer to some other ideas collected under the heading of Gnosticism, in which Sophia's error is not this quest for knowledge but the desire to imitate the Father by creating on her own. Without pretending that this tradition is the least bit unimportant, here I attempt only a reading of the knowledge-seeking story.

10 Brons undated d. Brons refers to Irenaeus 1992, 1.2.3, and Thomassen and Meyer 2007, 34.25-31.

11 Brons undated d, with reference to Irenaeus 1992, 1.2.4, and Hippolytus 1886, 31.5.

12 Irenaeus 1992, 1.4.1-2; Hippolytus 1886, 6.27; Thomassen 2007, 81.22-83.33. All referred to in Brons, undated d.

13 See Irenaeus 1992, 1.4.5; Hippolytus 1886, 6.27; Clement of Alexandria 1934, 43.2-45.2; Thomassen and Meyer 2007, 35-36; Thomassen 2007, 90.14f.

may not be especially negative.[14] First, matter provides a place for instruction, where the seeds of the spirit that Sophia has generated can take the necessary time to remember their divine source – just as Sophia had to do.[15] Memory is a crucial step toward gnosis, that is, knowing what one is and what is true. Second, and crucially, matter provides not just time, but helpful hints: Sophia works together with the descended savior to form matter into the image of the divine fullness, the All.[16] Matter calls to our memories with the voice of the divine. The redemptive knowledge in Valentinianism is knowing how to hear it.

Limits exist, then, between the One and the All, and between the All and the material world. The limits do not cross a vertical line, in the matter of the famous divided line of knowledge and reality in Plato's *Republic*.[17] Rather, they form concentric circles. A Valentinian limit does not close out, but seals within. As a generative restriction, Limit creates first the All of the Aeons, and then the realm of lower wisdom and matter, each in its way an image of the Father, though the images are not equally vivid.

Oddly enough, this insistence on the incomprehensible and provocative nature of matter is echoed in some contemporary philosophical movements, often in resistance to the view of matter that becomes particularly strong after the seventeenth century, holding that matter is inert, passive, and mechanical, awaiting human knowledge and action. What is called object- oriented ontology insists that objects – things, at any scale – not only evade full human comprehension, but trouble human supremacy, which we have based on our supposedly unique ability to know objects and act upon them.[18] Objects are not infinite, but their finitude and ours are mutually evasive, mutually limited: we cannot control them completely and we cannot know them completely. Humans are not uniquely agents in the world; objects act on us, too. There is an opacity to every object, a limit to every knowing.

The various ideas gathered under the heading of new materialism, on the other hand, emphasize the constant relations, even entanglements, among things.[19] Here the status of things is not more closed off than we had thought, but less individuated and

14 This is a matter of some argumentation, and of course either side – matter is an evil source of ignorance; matter offers a revelation – can be supported more or less from various texts. I do not pretend to offer here any sort of definitive claim, only one strand that I think can be followed through this strange and intriguing mode of thought.

15 Thomassen 2007, 122.32-123.22.

16 Ibid.

17 Plato 2008, 509D-511E.

18 The term "object-oriented philosophy" was coined by Graham Harman in 1999; see Harman, 2010, 93-104. According to Harman, the modification to "object-oriented ontology" comes from Levi Bryant. See "Series Editor's Introduction", in Bryant, 2014, ix. Both volumes provide useful introductions to the position and some of its variations.

19 The term "new materialism" is credited to independent coinages by Rosi Braidotti and Manuel DeLanda. See Braidotti 2000; DeLanda 1995. There are several good anthologies that provide introductions to the relevant range of ideas, including Dolphijn and van der Tuin 2012; Frost and Coole 2010; and in relation to theology, Keller and Rubenstein 2017.

self-contained. Here too, however, the impossibility of perfect knowing is central, now *because* of the extent of that interaction, and once more humans are not understood to be the world's only active beings; indeed, interactivity is complex and dazzling to the point of incomprehensibility.

These ideas are not cosmologies, nor do they have Valentinianism's self-consciously mythical poeticism. If anything, they reject myth in search of a rapport with post-Enlightenment science. But they do suggest that our understanding of objects and the ways in which we know them might move toward an unexpected common ground with the sense of the world as a place that harbors mystery. All three theories of existence lead us to suspect that the world is active upon us in ways that we do not always understand, and that even the world that we think we know often evades comprehension.

## Soteriology

As I have said, Limit functions redemptively as well as creatively; salvation is in knowing, and knowing comes through the power of Limit. Like lower wisdom, humanity is both comforted and taught by the Son's assistance – the Son, remember, who *is* Limit. For the Valentinians, Jesus, the personification of the son, really is a rabbi; he saves by teaching, and salvation is not atonement, but learning. (This is probably the primary tension between Gnostic Christianities and those that will become orthodoxy.) One of the key things that he teaches is how to read. This is particularly clear in the Gospel of Truth, which tells us:

> He came forward and uttered the word as a teacher. The self-appointed wise people came up to him, testing him, but he refuted them, for they were empty, and they despised him, for they were not truly intelligent.[20]

Valentinianism, like many other forms of Gnosticism, is strongly influenced by Platonic ideas, but the Platonic resonance here is somewhat unusual: in these actions the Son sounds very like Socrates, who famously questioned wise people, determined that they were never as wise as they thought they were, and realized that his own form of wisdom was the knowledge of limits – that is, the knowledge of how much he did not know.[21] Indeed, says Socrates, human wisdom is always limited, and it can never comprehend the ultimate, divine truth.[22] Socrates taught anyone who would listen to seek self-knowledge, which must include this knowledge of limitation. The Son teaches those who can hear him to read: "In their hearts," says the Gospel of Truth, "appeared the living book of the living, which is written in the father's thought and intellect. And since the foundation of the entirety it had been among his incomprehensibilities...."[23]

20 Layton 1987b, 19.17-26.
21 Plato 1996a, 21B-23A.
22 Plato, 1996a, 20D-20E and 23A.
23 Layton 1987b, 19.24-20.5. Ellipsis mine.

The audience learns to read, in other words, what cannot be comprehended, and they learn to read it within themselves, "in their hearts." Those whose opinion of their own human knowledge is too high will be shown to be foolish by this incomprehensible truth – a warning that Socrates and the Valentinians both take seriously. The first thing we must know is the limits of knowledge.

The strange living book of the living contains all the names of the saved. When the children of the father learn to read, they read their own names, which preexisted any individuated self. The "living enrolled in the book of the living," says the Gospel of Truth, "learn about themselves, recovering themselves from the Father, returning to him."[24]

Like matter in the image of the All, this book in which names are written is a reminder. So that it can be revealed, the book is bodily; "and no one had been able to take it up, inasmuch as it was ordained that whoever should take it up would be put to death. … Jesus appeared, wrapped himself in that document, was nailed to a piece of wood, and published the father's edict upon the cross."[25] An incarnate, materialized Son, wrapped in the skin-document of the living book, presents divinity so that material human beings can grasp it, learning through the senses. "Acquaintance from the father and the appearance of his son gave them a means to comprehend. For when they saw and heard him, he let them taste and smell himself and touch the beloved son…"[26] In the First Apocalypse of James, Jesus assures James, "I shall complete what is destined here on earth, as I once said from the heavens. And I shall reveal to you your deliverance."[27] This revelation requires careful attention to flesh, to what is "here on earth." Indeed, it requires that we attend to the limit or the boundary of flesh, to the skin, which serves as scripture's divine parchment. "Reading," the means of knowledge, is a way of seeing, hearing, touching – of sensing and interpreting, of responding to the call formed in the material world. The book can only be published in flesh – in matter, which can no longer be reductively understood.

Each reader of the book, reading her or his own name, reads the book itself. What is more, each reader is the flesh, the body as which the book is published. The reading and the fleshly being cannot be extricated from one another. David Brons explains, "the incarnation is … in effect the simultaneous redemption of all who are part of [Jesus's] body."[28] Who are these parts? Brons says, "the body of the human Jesus is consubstantial with the Church. According to Theodotus, 'the body of Jesus…was of the same substance as the Church'" (this is not an unorthodox claim, but the Valentinian spin on it does not become doctrine).[29] It is in the body that the divinity within each member is awakened, because each member of the church is a member of the divine body. The

24 Layton 1987b, 21.1-7.

25 Layton 1987b, 20.3-5, 20.26-27. Ellipsis mine.

26 Layton 1987b, 30.23-32. Ellipsis mine.

27 Funk 2007, 28.5-30.15.

28 Brons, undated a, with reference to Thomassen and Meyer 2007, 30: 28-30.

29 Brons, undated a. For the canonical version, see the Pauline first letter to the Corinthians, chapter 12. Brons also refers to the canonical books Romans 12:5, 1 Corinthians 12:12-13, Ephesians 4:16,

book and the flesh alike reveal the divine Father, but what they tell is unsayable, invisible, and incomprehensible.

The layering of levels here is extraordinary. The word and the body are there at the cross – not just *at* the limit, but *as* the Limit (who is the Son). The body on the cross is the published book; the book is the many-membered body of the church, containing all the members' names; and the Son, whose body it is, is the image of the Father, stretched out both to mark a limit and to draw back together. And those written in the book learn from it how to read themselves and the world in which they are already implicated. The body becomes a book, and the book a body: the word is made flesh, and it is published on a cross.[30]

This crucifixion is not merely an ending, of course – limitation must be more complex than that. All Christian notions of bodily resurrection are more or less weird. While many early Christians did believe that it was in some sense our presently lived flesh that rose, they also argued that it would, of necessity, be transformed – that it had to be changed if it was to be a place of pure joy and celebration.[31] The Valentinians think so too – but for them, again, the change is now, through learning, and not later, through atonement. With revelation, the person's experience of the body and the world it inhabits is transfigured; "and the world has already become the eternal realm," as the Gospel According to Philip declares.[32] Some of the Valentinian bodily metaphors are very much like those of orthodoxy: in the eucharist, for example, "one receives the spiritual flesh and blood of the resurrection body and becomes joined to the 'body of Christ.'"[33] What is missing is not the transfiguration of the flesh, but the end of the world, with its corresponding emphasis on afterward.

In a thoughtful essay on the Valentinian Treatise on Resurrection, Ryann Craig notes that even critics as harsh as Tertullian and Clement, two of the early church fathers who helped to shape orthodoxy, acknowledge that Valentinus believed in a flesh that

---

and Colossians 1:18, 2:19, as well as to Clement of Alexandria 1934, 42.3, 26.1, 17.1; Irenaeus 1992, 1.7.2, and Thomassen 2007, 122.12-17.

30 Here too there is an overlap with later canonical Christian scriptures. The fourth gospel in the Christian Bible includes the declaration "And the Word was made flesh, and dwelt among us" (John 1:14), NRSV.

31 See 1. Corinthians 15:50-52: "What I am saying, brothers and sisters, is this: flesh and blood cannot inherit the kingdom of God, nor does the perishable inherit the imperishable. Listen, I will tell you a mystery! We will not all die, but we will all be changed…and the dead will be raised imperishable, and we will be changed." NRSV. See also discussions in Irenaeus 1992, Book 5; Tertullian 2016; Augustine 2003, Book 23. Outi Lehtipuu (2015) notes the ways in which Valentinian texts, in particular, complicate any easy dichotomy between spirit and flesh. See especially 146n228; 153f. I am grateful to the anonymous manuscript reviewer who recommended this resource.

32 Layton 1987a, 86.11-14.

33 In Brons, undated c, citing Layton 1987a, 56.26-57.22. "And what, too, is this flesh that will inherit it (the Kingdom of God)? It is Jesus's flesh, along with his blood. It is necessary to arise in this kind of flesh, since everything exists in it." Layton 1987a, 56.24-57.1. My parenthesis.

was the same in Jesus as in the redeemed.[34] As Craig points out, "the [Treatise] does not indicate any special qualities differentiating Jesus' flesh from the flesh of general humanity."[35] That makes sense if each of the redeemed is also a member of the body of Christ, which is complete in every part. The disciple in the Treatise is reminded, "you received flesh when you entered this world. Why will you not receive flesh when you ascend into the Aeon?"[36] The ascent is a re-knowing – not a destruction. We reread the body, too, and we learn that it is more than we thought. In contemporary philosophy, 'flesh' is often used to indicate a complex, new materialist sense of mobile and interactive matter, on the basis that 'body' might imply solidity and self-sufficiency. In this sense, the Valentinian word embodied is decidedly a word made flesh. Language and body, in their very limitation, show us that from them and beyond them is more than we can know.

I have said something of the flesh, but word too is complicated in its limitation and containment. The living book contains all names, and several Valentinian texts suggest that the revelation is itself a name; indeed, that "the Name of the Father is the Son."[37] In the Gospel of Truth, we read, "It is he who in the beginning named what emanated from him, remaining always the same. And he begot him as a son and gave him his name, which he possessed."[38] The Tripartite Tractate tells us, "He manifested [himself], though he cannot be spoken."[39] The name is paradoxical, at once revealed and unsayable.[40]

In many esoteric traditions, names are powerful, and are often associated with creation, where a thing comes to be by virtue of being named. Theodotus describes the Valentinian baptismal rite as the receipt of an angelic name, which pairs the human soul to its companion angel. These angels are less independent entities than aspects of Christ; they are another version of the Aeons. Thus, this joining in name echoes the membership in the body: the named human takes on an aspect of the divine, as the (baptized) member of the church becomes a member – a limb or a piece – of the divine body.[41] Theodotus writes:

---

34 Craig cites Attridge 1985, n. 38, pp. 146-47.

35 Craig 2012, 487. Craig cites Treatise on the Resurrection 44.21-26; 45.25-26; 46.16-17.

36 Treatise on the Resurrection 47.2-8, cited in Craig 2012, 491.

37 Layton 1987b, 38.6.

38 Layton 1987b, 38.6-12.

39 Thomassen 2007, 72.

40 The Gospel According to Philip provides further complexity. "'Jesus' is a private name," it says; "'Christ' (the anointed) is a public name. … 'The Nazarene' is the public name of the private name." Layton 1987a, 56.3-13. Parenthesis original, ellipsis mine. This gospel also links the doubleness of names to the above and below marked out by the cross: "'Father' and 'son' are simple names; 'holy spirit' is a two-part name. For they exist everywhere—above, below; in the hidden, in the visible." Layton 1987a, 59.11-18.

41 Brons undated d. "The Savior is associated with a retinue of angels who are the prototypes of the spiritual element present in every Christian. Like rays of the sun, they are not distinct or self-sufficient individuals. Rather, they represent the dynamic richness of Jesus." Brons cites Irenaeus 1992, 1.2.6 and Clement of Alexandria, 1934, 39-40.

> when we, too, have the Name, we may not be hindered and kept back by the Limit and the Cross from entering the [All]. Wherefore, at the laying on of hands they say at the end, 'for the angelic redemption' that is, for the one which the angels also have, in order that the person who has received the redemption may be baptised in the same Name in which his angel had been baptised before him.

Human and angel, human and divine aspect, are joined by being given a joint name.[42] Moreover, they are given that joint name by a touch between bodies, specifically by the laying on of hands, bringing the word and the flesh together once more.

The names do not all merge into one name, yet each is contained in the other. The angels are aspects of the Son, and the Son is the name of the Father. According to Irenaeus, Valentinus's disciple Marcus amplifies this theme, by identifying the Aeons with the letters of the name. "So the pronunciation of the whole name consisted of thirty letters, but four combinations (of letters). Each of the characters had its own letters, its own impressions, its own pronunciation, shape, and images; and not one of them [characters] perceives the form of that [combination] of which it is a character."[43] The Aeons, like letters, do not know what words they spell. Like us, they are ignorant of the full name.[44] We read in the Gospel of Truth about that "higher redemption," the one that we join by joining names:

> For he revealed it to bestow an acquaintance in harmony with all its emanations, that is to say, acquaintance with the living book, and acquaintance which at the end appeared to the aeons in the form of [passages of text from] it. When it is manifest, they speak: they are not places for use of the voice, nor are they mute texts for someone to read out and so think of emptiness; rather, they are texts of truth, which speak and know only themselves. And each text is a perfect truth—like a book that is perfect and consists of texts written in unity, written by the father for the aeons, so that through its passages of text the aeons might become acquainted with the father.[45]

The book is perfect in each letter, complete, even though no letter knows what it says. The body is complete in each member, though no member knows the whole of the sacred flesh. The instructed reader's attention is drawn not to the abstract concept, but

---

42 Clement of Alexandria 1934, 22.

43 Irenaeus 1992, 1.14.1. Parenthesis mine.

44 See Brons undated b. "This astonishing idea has its root in the notion that the emanation of the Name by the Father was a process of self-limitation. Valentinus himself admits that it is an surprising idea, 'It was quite amazing that they were in the Father without being acquainted with him and that they alone were able to emanate, inasmuch as they were not able to perceive and recognize the one in whom they were.' The Aeons can be thought of as unintegrated aspects of the Son's overall personality who are unaware of the Name even while they form part of it." Citing Layton 1987b, 22.

45 Layton 1987b, 22.35-23.17.

to the matter of words, the very letters making up the name from which all names are drawn. This name is knowable only when only when brought before the senses – and yet, at the same time, it remains incomprehensible and unpronounceable. The mode of truth here, the way in which the Son as name and body is the image of truth, is holographic. That is, in each bit, the whole image is present: the whole body in each member, the whole book in each letter, the whole name in each name. A smaller piece of a hologram gives us a somewhat smudged, less vivid image than a larger piece does, but each fragment contains the whole image nonetheless. What makes this particularly fascinating here is that the image can only be what it is insofar as it has each part; that is, it is not the image of an undifferentiated blob.[46]

Matter is formed in that image; when we learn to read the divine in the material world, the divine image shows forth. Learning will begin at baptism, when a person is joined to the community of the church, becomes the same flesh as that divine body, and receives a name that is one of the letters that fully contains the holy name. The name teaches reading, and what is read is the name. We do not find that flesh and meaning are separate here, that human intelligence gives meaningfulness to the passive inanimate world. Not only are meaningful word and flesh utterly entangled, each is also complete in the smallest part. There is a strong resonance with contemporary philosophies of materiality in the insistence on the world's agency and the giving of meaning as an act not restricted to humankind; there is, however, a difference as well, in this particular strangeness of part and whole, and of course in the cosmology giving rise to it. What is within and without, contained by limit or cut away by it, teaches us of the other.

## Evocation

For a redemption by knowledge, all of this revelation is nonetheless weirdly elusive. Names may designate; that is, they may point out what they name, or pick it out of a group. This name does not seem to be a very good designator, because if it were, it would give us reasonably certain knowledge of the thing that it names, of an object or person's identity. Instead, it seems to pick out everything and nothing. But names do something else too: they call. This name calls everything; it is written by the All as itself/themselves; it is written by the Father as the Son. The world in its form calls to us, enchants us, reveals to us more than can be said. It is perhaps surprising to read an echo of this esoteric claim in conflicting contemporary paradigms of materiality. Jane Bennett, generally identified as a new materialist, tells us that she wonders "whether the very characterization of the world as disenchanted ignores and then discourages

46 There is an even earlier precedent for this holographic reality, though we do not have evidence that the Valentinians knew of it. The Presocratic philosopher Anaxagoras (fifth century BCE) argued that "all is in all," and that the usual distinctions of mixture and separation were misconceived. An early account of his philosophy is available in Diogenes Laërtius 2014, 2.6-15. What remains of Anaxagoras's own work is available in a translation with commentary by Patricia Curd, Anaxagoras 2010.

affective attachment to that world. The question is important because the mood of enchantment may be valuable for ethical life." To be enchanted, she explains, is "to be struck and shaken by the extraordinary that lives amid the familiar and the everyday."[47] The approach that she encourages, for ethical and political reasons, demands that we be susceptible to this call of the extraordinary, rather than resisting or ignoring it by insisting upon its mundane character. Bennett, to be sure, is firmly opposed to allowing theology into this delight: "My quasi-pagan model of enchantment pushes against a powerful and versatile Western tradition (in the disciplines of history, philosophy, and literature) that make enchantment depend on a divine creator, Providence, or, at the very least, a physical world with some original connection to a divine will."[48] And Graham Harman, the prototypical object-oriented ontologist, asks,

> Will philosophy remain satisfied with not addressing any of these objects by name, so as to confine itself to a 'more general' discussion of the condition of the condition of the condition of possibility of ever referring to them? ...Or is there some possibility of an object-oriented philosophy, a sort of alchemy for describing the transformation of one entity into another, for outlining the ways in which they seduce or destroy humans and non-humans alike? [I] endorse[] the latter option.[49]

The seductiveness or destructiveness of things lies, in no small measure, in the ways in which they call to us. In their very different fashions, these two figures within these diverse materialist movements echo the enticement, the evocation, by which the Valentinians heard the divine name calling in the book and the body both; that is, in the very world rightly read. The gods to which the contemporary philosophers object, with their omnipotent distance from the world, are not the divinity that the Father's children read in the smallest thing.

So the body of the name may, in its enticement, call us in surprisingly anachronistic ways. But here another puzzle intrudes: why does the Father need something else to be its name at all? Another way to ask this question might be: why would the One create Limit? We read in the Valentinian Exposition that the father "exists as Oneness, [being alone] in silence – 'silence' means tranquility – since [he was] in fact One, and nothing existed before him. He also exists [as] Twoness and as a pair – his partner is Silence."[50] Silence at the start, in the Monad and the Pair, thinks itself, as we saw in Valentinian cosmology, and thus "God [came] forth, the Son, Mind of All." "This, then, [is the] root [of] the All, Oneness before whom there is no one; [he is also] Twoness, dwelling in Silence and speaking only with himself...."[51] The Gospel of Truth adds,

47 Bennett 2001, 3-4.

48 Bennett 2001, 12.

49 Harman 2010, 95.

50 Thomassen and Meyer 2007, 22.

51 Thomassen and Meyer 2007, 22-23. My ellipsis. The Untitled Tractate that David Brakke discusses in his consideration of Gnostic body and boundary makes a similar claim, as he writes: "the

"Since the time when they constituted the depth of his thought, uttered discourse has manifested them, and intellect uttering the discourse, and silent loveliness."[52] Silence befits what cannot be captured by words, but silence without speech is as meaningless as an uninterrupted buzz of sound. Silence is in the word and the word in silence, and it is only thus that the name can call, or be called. The Father, dwelling in depth and silence, needs a name.

It is important that this call transforms, but does not deny, the world. Like some other forms of Gnosticism, Valentinianism is not especially interested in life *after* death, in a disembodied time to come. And like the better-known Thomas Christians, it holds that "God is near at hand, and not far off."[53] Valentinus says of the baptized, "And it is in them that the father dwells, and in the father that they are..."[54] Both suggest an immanent divinity, but not a contained one: each is in each. Yet Christian authors who wrote against what they saw as heresies resoundingly condemned Gnostic Christianities, even Valentinianism, for their *rejection* of flesh, for identifying matter with ignorance – as that *from* which we require redemption.[55] The transformation in the view of the world is read, then, as an insistence that this world is illusory and even contemptible. I would not argue that this reading is baseless, but in some Gnostic variations, I do think that a more world-positive reading is possible. There may be a parallel in contemporary materialisms' frequent beginning in hostility toward philosophy's twentieth-century "linguistic turn," understood as the move away from an interest in things and matter and toward language alone, even to the point of declaring that things are made by discourse about them. In what is called the "material turn," language's formative role is firmly rejected, on the grounds that it paid no attention to real material conditions, and matter, however mute, is regarded as having agency. The proto-orthodox criticism seems similar: that is, because the Gnostic variations emphasize knowing, spirit, and the error of perceiving matter simplistically (or reductively) as everything, Gnostic Christianities are criticized as having rejected the material world altogether. The inextricability of flesh from word, however, suggests that it is misplaced – and that neither language nor matter, sense nor sensing, can successfully turn all the way from the other.

## One, another

We have already seen that for the Valentinians, being in a material body gives the spirit time to learn and remember, and that the material world is shaped to prompt that remembrance: it is, rather literally, a form of divinity (that is, it is in the form of the divine). Matter may spring from suffering, but it is the image of joy. Redemption is

---

Father whose spoken word penetrates both upper and lower regions is also a spring that pours forth silence." Brakke 2009, 212.

52 Layton 1987b, 37.7-12.

53 Pearson 2007, 115.10-23.

54 Layton 1987b, 42.46-47.

55 See Tertullian 2016, 16.

neither at a later time nor in another place, but here, and now. The Limit, which imposes unknowing, is also what reveals: the body and the name of the Son reveal the inconceivable Father. At the crucifixion as the Gospel of Truth describes it, what we think of as limitations – death as the limit of life, ignorance as the limit of knowing – are undone. This does not mean that they turn into their opposites. The limit of knowing does not somehow reveal unlimited comprehension. The death on the cross does not extend life limitlessly into time. But this is because the unlimited is not the opposite of limit.

Rather, what we learn is that the other is one and one is other. Knowledge is limited, and thinking by itself does not reach the One. This does not mean that there are more facts, with which we are currently unacquainted. It means that there is something that pulls at our desire to know, but is other than knowledge without being outside of it. Sophia's problem was that she thought the inconceivable One was a thing that she could think, and reach by thinking alone. But what else is there? The strangeness of matter is met by equal strangeness in knowing.

Oddly enough, we can actually clarify some of this with a brief detour through some of the weirdest and most confusing parts of Platonism, the late dialogues and the unwritten doctrines. One of the reasons that Plato's divided line from the *Republic*, a middle-period dialogue, became so famous is that it lines up ontology on one side and epistemology on the other. Existing things and the ways in which we know them are ordered in tidy pairs. True knowledge belongs to the intellectual realm, and opinion to the visible realm, where the constant transformation of things keeps us from certainty. In Valentinus's radiant cosmological circles, ontology and epistemology also work together. In the ways in which world and knowing interact, we will find a startlingly contemporary resonance, but we must find it through a quite different aspect of Plato's thought.

In many of his late dialogues, Plato argues that knowledge is a matter of collection and division. We must know how to tell apart things that are different from one another, and we must know what things should be gathered together. (Already we can hear the resonance of the Valentinian puzzles of oneness and difference.) The point first emerges in the *Phaedrus* – in which, uniquely, Socrates ventures outside the limiting wall of his beloved Athens. Here, Socrates declares that we must divide topics "where the natural joints are, and not trying to break any part, after the manner of a bad carver… just as the body, which is one, is naturally divisible into two, right and left."[56] Some version of this claim emerges again and again in dialogues including the *Theaetetus,* the *Statesman,* and the *Parmenides*. But it never seems to work – the arguments contradict themselves, or multiple entities appear with the same name, or the same appearance; even Forms start multiplying out of control.[57]

---

56 Plato 1995a, 265E-266A.

57 In the *Theaetetus*, one character is a bright young man from Athens who is not very good-looking, but resembles Socrates. Plato 2014, 143C-144A. In the *Statesman*, one of Socrates' young interlocutors shares his name. Plato 1995b, 257C. In the *Parmenides*, the theory of Forms becomes entangled by the impossibility of including a Form within the set of things of which it is a Form. Plato 1996b, 128Eff.

If we do not assume that Plato was simply losing his intellectual powers late in life, then it must be that he was neither confused about nor blind to the tensions and contradictions in these texts. What if this consideration of what to include and exclude is actually meant to show us how strange and unknowable these limits really are? Some scholars have considered the possibility that traces of Plato's unwritten teachings actually make their way into some of the late writings, usually indirectly.[58] This might account for some of the confusing parts.

Saying that Plato had unwritten teachings sounds like the sort of conspiracy theory about ancient, hidden wisdom that the Internet loves, very like the use that popular culture makes of Gnosticism. But we actually have evidence from Aristotle, in his *Physics* and *Metaphysics*; from one of his students, who describes Plato's very weird public lecture on "the Good" that turned out to be about number; and from works by some of Plato's own students and successors, which pick up on some of the same ideas that Aristotle describes.[59]

The heart of the unwritten doctrines is that the beginning of all is a pair: the One and the Indefinite Dyad, which generate everything else that is.[60] The terminology for this primal pair is inconsistent: the One is also called Unity and Limit, and the Dyad is also called the Indefinite Two, the Great and the Small, and the Unlimited. The One gives the Dyad definition: *by limiting it,* making difference within it. That is: it is the One, undifferentiated, that generates difference, within the Dyad, which is two and thus differentiated, but indefinite and thus undifferentiated. The One must have within it the power of not-One. The indefinite Dyad must have within it the potential, the potency, for definition. Within each is the condition of its own other.[61] Within each is itself. Within each is the whole, which is made of itself and its other.

The puzzles of collection and division begin to make a paradoxical kind of sense. When we collect or gather together, we are performing two actions: drawing into one, and excluding all others. But the One cannot exclude any others, since exclusion always makes two. When we divide, we distinguish one from another, but the principle of division, or limit, belongs only to the (unlimited) One; it can never be included within the categories that it makes. In other words, the confusion induced by the late dialogues might be a hint to us that when we collect and divide, when we think delimitation and unlimitedness, we really do generate and encounter paradox, but this paradox is not mere nonsense.

---

58 Important voices here include Sayre 1983 and Miller 1995. There is one fairly direct mention, in the *Philebus*, of a kind of being that is both limited and unlimited at once. Plato 1993, 27B-27C.

59 Aristotle 2008, 209b13–15; 1993, 987b20-22 and 988a10-15. The student who describes the lecture is Aristoxenus 1902.

60 Aristotle 1993, 988a10-15, and Theophrastus 2010, 6b10-15.

61 Cf. Turner: "Then I ascended to the Vitality as I sought it. I mutually entered it and stood, not firmly but quietly. And I saw an eternal, intellectual, undivided motion, all-powerful, formless, unlimited by limitation." 60.20-29.

To explore this paradoxical sense, let us return to Valentinianism. Remember, the Valentinian version of limit does not divide lines; it inscribes circles within circles. Rather than excluding, it encloses more tightly. The All is in the illimitable One by limitation. The One, like Plato's One, generates Limit and definition, creating inside of what can have no outside, as its own other. Collection and division cannot be opposed here. *Knowledge* in the sense of information *is* about collection and division, about knowing the natural places to cut, or knowing what kinds of categorization are useful for different purposes. The limit, as the place that is neither collected nor divided, as the source of creation and revelation, of cutting-off and unknowing, cannot belong to knowledge. And yet knowing *can* include the knowledge *that* the limit *is*. That is, we can know, like Socrates, that our knowledge is limited. In the *Symposium*, Socrates uses the voice of the prophetess Diotima to describe a love beyond philosophy (philosophy is the love of Sophia, of wisdom). The higher love takes as its object no part of a body, no item of knowledge, no thing. What it desires is in no place, at no time; its object is simply Beauty.[62] Knowledge is drawn beyond itself by *Eros*, by desirous love.

The thought of the unthinkable One makes two, Father and Son. But the two are One; there is nothing between them. Indeed, there is no division that does not contain wholeness. When the name of the Father, the Son, is called out, it calls both, the One and the Pair. This means that our binaries do not stay neatly apart. For the Valentinians, ascent is a deeper immanence, a deeper other-in-oneness. Silence must permeate language, so that we can read sense. Infinity must permeate skin-bounded flesh, so that matter can live. Deep in the depthless limit, not across it, is the divine that is depth and silence.

Obviously, a perfect, stable fusion of all of these opposites is impossible. But Einar Thomassen, discussing the Tripartite Tractate, reminds us that "the [all] does not exist as a static structure but as a process, whose directing goal is knowledge of the Father, and unity, both with the object known and internal unity. But because the aeons are endowed with the freedom of will this unity must remain a potentiality and the process an unending one."[63] That is, their will cannot be altogether subsumed to the will of the Father, even though they are also not other than he is. And they cannot know entirely, even though they are not wholly other than the known. And we too ascend, in gloriously re-written flesh, into the All; or rather, we recognize that we have ascended, into the depth of the world, into the holographic all in all, where the world enchants us, and an epistemic alchemy shows the divinity even of dirt.

To think of the limits of our thinking, we must think of the beginning. In the beginning is the One. And the One thinks the thought of itself, and generates the Son, the Limit. But this thinking is not knowledge, which was not lacking. We might now suspect what can lead us past knowing: Hippolytus tells us in *The Refutation of All Heresies* that despite the peaceful quiet, "(the Father) was not fond of solitariness. For… He was all

62 Plato 1989, 21A-21C.

63 Thomassen 1980. He continues, "This is apparently what is meant by 'the Limit' which causes them to be silent about the Father but to speak of their desire to know him (75.13-17, cf. 72.25-27)."

love, but love is not love except there may be some object of affection."[64] The world comes to be in love thinking itself in order to have something to love. Desire moves only within difference. This is why the One, which imposes Limit, creates difference in the process; this is why the unlimited Dyad accepts limitation. And the two work together in the completeness and incompletion of the world. As Diotima told Socrates, it is eros that moves further than wisdom.

If we perceive the Limit intellectually, it is a barrier, as it was at first to Sophia. To thinking without desire, material bodies stand in the way of spiritual knowing, and human language stands in the way of true names. But this is wisdom, too – to know that there is a limit to what we can comprehend. At the limit, desire moves. When we read the world rightly, it speaks to us: we realize that reminders of divinity are everywhere, and we too can fall in love, can be enchanted and seduced by Beauty.

In the Gospel of Truth, we read, "from the moment that the father is known the lack will not exist."[65] Incompleteness does not exist, not because everything has become indifferent, but because every fragment is also complete. At each moment, the world is holographic. As a process, we might imagine it as fractal, each unfolding of a whole a new whole in itself. Completeness does not rest, because the truth in every bit is a paradox, and paradoxes are mobile. The Limit looks like a boundary, like a limitation or a barrier, when we perceive it with logic alone. But limiting knowledge, it sustains desire. The Valentinian Exposition tells us that the Son "is the producer of the All and the actualization [of the thought] of the Father – which is [Desire]."[66] The Aeons exist in order to love, because they are loved; they must, to love, to desire, remain other than the One.[67]

When we perceive limit with both knowledge and desire, it becomes revelation.[68] The anonymous medieval *Book of the 24 Philosophers* offers a definition of God as "an infinite sphere, whose center is everywhere (and) circumference is nowhere,"[69] a definition that later mystics take up with pleasure. Much earlier, the limit of the Valentinians encircles nothing; everywhere is its center, and in every center its God is whole. In every letter, in every atom, there is the truth of divinity, of the multiplicity of one, of the unity of two.

The Limit stops our comprehension, but by doing so, it enables our desire. In this pairing, our spirit moves like the One. The Limit is revelation not of a body that is outside of our senses (somewhere in the ultraviolet range of light or subsonic sound waves, perhaps); not of a name that points us to a new thing (like a word learned for a

---

64 Hipppolytus 1886, 219.

65 Layton 1987b, 24.29-32.

66 Thomassen and Meyer 2007, 24.

67 See Thomassen 2007, 71.

68 In the *Philebus*, Socrates argues that the best life belongs to the category of things that are at once limited and unlimited, and that it is a mix of pleasure and wisdom. If we grant that pleasure is desire's object, we see how closely the cosmology follows this late line of Platonic thought. Plato 1993, 27C-27E.

69 "Deus est sphaera infinita cuius centrum est ubique, circumferential nusquam." Anonymous 1997.

novel object or in a foreign language); not of facts of which we must remain perpetually ignorant – but of bodily infinity that has meaning, the name of silence that has body, the 'knowledge' of mystery: of what is, already, immanent. The letters of the name spell out the body, the body that puts on the book. The stretch of the body on the cross publishes the name.

In the epistemology of desire and thought, thinking desires completion: it seeks to comprehend and to be comprehensive. Desire knows incompletion: it must sustain its reaching. Desire generates more knowledge by always going further. Knowledge generates more desire by finding out new objects. The ontology that belongs to this pair is one of paradox: of pairs that both are and only seem to be different, like the Aeons in the All. And it is an ontology of completeness in each fragment, which does not undo the fragments' difference.

As we in the humanities work to take materiality seriously, we have tended to push away both words and gods, both the linguistic and the divine. Harman argues that we must resist modernity's confidence in our knowledge and control of objects; Bennett cautions us against allowing our view of modernity as disenchanted to disenchant our world in turn. For both, as for many modern and postmodern thinkers, theology could only be about a divinity that imposes control, fixity, and finality upon the cosmos, and anthropocentrism upon our part of the world. And of all theological variants, the Christian God must surely be the worst instance of these tendencies. Valentinianism is among the many versions of early Christianity to tell us otherwise. Here the necessity of the Longed-For as consort to Wisdom, of the Dyad as other within the One, of openness to the image told only in the world as the way of reading the Word, all give us an interactive, seductive, and enchanted cosmos. It cannot be dematerialized. In every bit of what is, everything is; and everything is meaningful, corporeal, bound, and illimitable, and made so by Limit. The revelation continues to unveil. The world acts, and we in it: it offers the image of desire, in all the multiplicity of its movements, and it is near at hand, and not far off.

# DECOLONIZING ANCIENT SEXUALITY

## Three Case Studies

JONATHAN CAHANA-BLUM

**ABSTRACT** *By analyzing the we–they paradigm premised in three influential scholarly analyses of ancient sexuality, I exemplify how modern scholars tend to colonize the ancient as primitive, position themselves as interpreters, and uncritically embody an ideal Western subject. Such a discourse ends in reifying both the primitivism of Mediterranean antiquity and the superiority of the Western modern subject. It thus tends to distort both views, co-opting itself into a dangerous modern colonial project. On the micro-level, such an approach often results in a hidden misogyny being applied to the interpretation of the ancient text, so as to fit the expectations of the colonizer.*

## Introduction

Methodologically aware studies of ancient sexuality, however precisely defined, have tended to emphasize the difference between modernity, as inhabited and experienced by the respective scholar, and antiquity. Initially, this was a highly beneficial corrective to earlier scholarship, which tended to assume that modern Western sexual concepts are universal. Nevertheless, it has also, more often than not, applied a we–they paradigm that either uncritically accepts modernity's public claims about itself, or assumes the primitivity of antiquity. Both introduce a highly treacherous pitfall into scholarship and risk becoming part of a dangerous colonial project, whether intended by the scholar or inoculated into their rhetoric inadvertently.

Such an approach is especially hazardous when present in basic and highly influential studies of ancient sexuality, through which both students and more established scholars are initiated into the field, and which otherwise include many pertinent and crucial methodological considerations that are highly useful for understanding premodern sexuality. Thus, in this essay I would like to address three such studies: David Halperin's *One Hundred Years of Homosexuality*, Dale Martin's *The Queer History of Galatians 3:28*, and Daniel Boyarin's *Gender*.[1] In each case it will be seen that the problem lies in a (probably inadvertent) colonial approach that uncritically accepts modernity's concept of itself and its inherent superiority to primitive Mediterranean antiquity, and thus distorts our understanding of both modernity and antiquity. My own method is rather straightforward: I will counterpoise the above-mentioned studies with feminist and queer research into modern sexualities. It will then be clear how such studies' reliance

1 Halperin 1990; Martin 2006, 77-90; Boyarin 1998.

on modernity is at odds with the critical studies of the latter have produced. In other words, to paraphrase a well-known title, we have never really been modern.[2]

## David Halperin and Sexual Politics

Halperin's collection of essays *One Hundred Years of Homosexuality*, and especially the titular article, have been highly influential both within and outside of classics. Many of Halperin's points are now taken as almost self-evident, as a recent collection clearly demonstrates.[3] Yet its problematic unawareness of modern sexual politics has not been sufficiently addressed.[4] This could be done by comparing Halperin's methodical assumptions about modern sexuality with Kate Millet's *Sexual Politics*, a manifesto of second-wave feminism that was published a full twenty years before Halperin's study.[5]

In demonstrating why it would be futile to identify and analyze the "sexuality" of the ancient Greeks, Halperin argues the following:

> When the sexual system of the classical Athenians is described in that fashion, as though it constituted a separate sphere of life governed by its own internal laws, it appears merely exotic or bizarre … But if, instead of treating Athenian sexual attitudes and practices as expression of ancient Greek "sexuality" (conceived, in modern terms, as an autonomous domain), we situate them in the larger social context in which they are embedded, they will at once disclose their systematic coherence. For the "sexuality" of the classical Athenians, far from being independent and detached from "politics" *(as we conceive sexuality to be)*, was constituted by the very principles on which Athenian public life was organized. … Sex in classical Athens, then, was not simply a collaboration in some private quest for mutual pleasure that absorbed or obscured, if only temporarily, the social identities of its participants.[6]

There is little point in trying to challenge Halperin's argument about ancient Greek sexuality. There his claim is thoroughly sound. The problem lies precisely in the (highly explicit) we–they paradigm he employs in order to demarcate it. In modernity, we are requested to assume, sex is non-political – but a private quest for mutual pleasure that allows us to experience, if only momentarily, a true egalitarian relationship between (or, probably more crucial for Halperin's argument, also within) the sexes. Not so among

2 Cf. Latour 1993.

3 Blondell and Ormand 2015.

4 Sha 2006 has addressed Halperin's politics of difference, and the way it is used to valorize a modern homosexuality in which gender plays no role (cf. esp. 46). Halperin 2015 was written partly as a rejoinder to this criticism. For further discussion, see below.

5 Millet 2000 (originally published in 1969).

6 Halperin 1990, 31-32, emphasis mine.

the primitive in ancient Greece, where sex was political and politics was sexual, always working to ensure the stratification of power relations in society.[7]

While Western modernity would certainly like to present itself this way – and such a rhetoric has frequently been used to advance different colonial projects – Kate Millet has been pioneering in demonstrating its falsity. She further argued that it was precisely such pretenses that had thwarted the first wave of feminist activism from effecting a true sexual revolution that would emancipate more than half of humanity. According to Millet, the argument that sex is a private quest that has no political consequences, and thus is not in any need of reform, has kept in place the most hideously basic tool of patriarchy to subjugate women: intercourse itself. Millet further argues:

> Coitus can scarcely take place in a vacuum; although of itself it appears a biological and physical activity, it is set so deeply within the larger context of human affairs that it serves as a charged microcosm of the variety of attitudes and values to which culture subscribes. Among other things, it may serve as a model of sexual politics on an individual or personal plane.[8]

In the postscript of her book, Millet does long for a time in which sex could be detached from politics, but I do not believe Halperin is working on the assumption that we are already there.[9] On the contrary, I am quite convinced that he is aware of modern sexual politics, but in his attempt to stress the difference between antiquity and modernity, the critical view of the latter inadvertently slides out of view. Indeed, as he himself admits in a much later article, the fact that sex is political is actually a similarity between antiquity and modernity, and in both cases the respective subjects would not necessarily be aware of sexual politics in each and every case they either witness or practise it:

---

7 Halperin stresses this very point of alleged difference between modernity and antiquity in order to advance the claim that modern homosexuality is an egalitarian *el dorado*. This has already been addressed by Sha 2006, 46. As is clear from the way my argument proceeds, this is but a symptom of the larger colonial we–they paradigm Halperin employs.

8 Millet 2000, 23. Millet demonstrates exactly how this works by analyzing its literary manifestations in the likes of D. H. Lawrence, Henry Miller, Norman Mailer, and Jean Genet. Her analysis of the latter is especially pertinent to our discussion, as it exemplifies the "painstaking exegesis of the barbarian vassalage of the sexual orders, the power structure of 'masculine' and 'feminine' as revealed by a homosexual, criminal world that mimics with brutal frankness the bourgeois heterosexual society" (18-19). The way that intercourse effects the politics of subordination has been further detailed in Dworkin 1987.

9 Millet 2000, 363: "It may be that a second wave of the sexual revolution might at last accomplish its aim of freeing half the race from its immemorial subordination – and in the process bring us all a great deal closer to humanity. It may be that we shall even be able to retire sex from the harsh realities of politics, but not until we have created a world we can bear out of the desert we inhabit."

> Sexual relations for many people in the ancient world, as for many people in the modern world, were surely not *about* power, penetration, or hierarchy, but they were nevertheless organized and *structured*, then as now, by differences between sexual partners in power, status, age, and sexual role.[10]

One could hardly agree more, but considering that the earlier work was and is the influential and formative one, and that this apparent retraction is not presented as such nor does it explicitly refer to his problematic claims in *One Hundred Years of Homosexuality*, Halperin's 1990 article continues to promulgate its colonial we–they politics. Nor does it help that even in his 2015 article Halperin is still not explicit enough on the effect sex has in *structuring* and *supporting* politics, in antiquity as in modernity. While in each case a different kind of politics is effected, the very fact that sex was never and – Millet's optimistic hopes voiced almost 50 years ago notwithstanding – will probably never be detached from politics is beyond any reasonable doubt.

### Dale Martin's *Queer History* and Sexual Equality

First published in English in his collection *Sex and the Single Savior*, Dale Martin's *The Queer History of Galatians 3:28* lucidly exemplifies how a we–they rhetoric may hamper an otherwise sound methodological approach to the history of exegesis. Martin's main point in this essay is that despite a feminist trend in modern exegesis arguing that Galatians 3:28 advances sexual equality, this could not have been what the verse meant to its original audience.[11] On the contrary, argues Martin, Paul's proclamation that "in Christ" there is no male or female "promised abolition of dimorphic sexuality, not sexual equality."[12] Moreover, this abolition was to be effected through a non-egalitarian androgyny, in which "the imperfect female was subsumed into the perfect male."[13] However, "we" in modernity can and should read it through our more egalitarian and enlightened eyes, and thus see Paul's proclamation as supporting "a symbiosis in which neither side has any reality or meaning apart from the equal, complementary play of the other."[14]

As a whole, Martin's arguments constitute a methodological minefield that has to be discharged carefully, even more so since Martin himself is well aware of both second-wave and third-wave feminism. Indeed, in a footnote, Martin argues that he rejects "second-wave feminist differentiation between 'gender' ... and 'sex.' I insist that biology *is* cultural and that culture *is* biological."[15] Yet it is important to practise what

10 Halperin 2015, 319. Emphasis original.

11 Quoted in full, Galatians 3:28 addresses other social and cultural divisions as well: "There is neither Jew nor Greek, there is neither slave nor free, there is neither male nor female; for you are all one in Christ Jesus."

12 Martin 2006, 87.

13 Martin 2006, 89; see also 84.

14 Martin 2006, 89.

15 Martin 2006, 220 n. 41.

one preaches, in antiquity as well as in modernity, and this third-wave feminist notion would necessarily preclude any pretense of "sexual equality" being oxymoronic or even downright deceptive. If sex is culturally constructed, it is so for a reason, and this reason has very little to do with equality. From such a perspective, which Martin himself argues is crucial to his approach, it would be highly problematical to argue that a certain verse proclaims the "abolition of dimorphic sexuality, not sexual equality." If both gender and sex are culturally constructed, it is precisely through the abolition of dimorphic sexuality (or the queering of the sex/gender system, to use a more modern terminology) that something like equality can be achieved. Indeed, it is as a luminous pioneer of third-wave feminism that Judith Butler argued that "discursive ordering and production of bodies in accord with the category of sex is itself a material violence" and that "If there is a fear that, by no longer being able to take for granted the subject, its gender, its sex, or its materiality, feminism will founder, it might be wise to consider the political consequences of keeping in their place the very premises that have tried to secure our subordination from the start."[16]

Of course, it is perfectly acceptable to reject Judith Butler's argument or even third-wave feminism as a whole. Many have, and the aforementioned quotation comes from Butler's rejoinder to those who did. But it is *not* acceptable to adopt Butler's argument and simultaneously reject Paul's proclamation of the end of sexual dimorphism as not advancing equality, unless one adopts a we–they approach that does not allow the primitive Mediterranean mind to advance to the height of Western thought. Moreover, Martin's adjacent argument that ancient androgyny is not egalitarian, since femaleness is subsumed by the male, yet "we" may read it today as complementary and thus egalitarian, only adds insult to the injury. First, the destruction of femaleness as an abusive construct made to subjugate those designated through it appears in modern feminism as well. One need only be reminded of radical feminist Ti-Grace Atkinson's powerful address to "women" that "you'll be afraid you'll die, and the woman will die, but your life will be born, and you'll begin to be free."[17] Second, ancient androgyny was much more complicated than Martin allows. While there are some cases of masculinizing the feminine, in others we find the exact opposite, as well as a thorough "queering" of both in a constant fluctuating interrelationship.[18] Third, Martin's advocation of a mod-

---

16 Butler 1995, 52; 54.

17 Atkinson 1974, 7.

18 The two latter options are especially pertinent in gnostic writings. For detailed discussion, see Cahana-Blum 2018, 80-98. As an aside, it is important to note that Martin also (mis)applies such a we–they approach to earlier scholarship, notably Laqueur 1990; he notes that "according to Laqueur, the modern body is a two-sexed body: male and female are taken to be different, and relatively equal, side of a dichotomy" (Martin 2006, 83-84). Nothing could be further from the truth. What Laqueur demonstrated in his book is that in the premodern one-sex system, feminine inferiority could be based on metaphysics, while in the modern two-sex system, it could be based on biology. In no way was the later system inherently more egalitarian than the earlier. Epistemology changed, and both sides now based their arguments on the body, with those arguing on the side of female inferiority certainly dominating the scene for quite some time. Cf. also

ern "enlightened" reading of ancient androgyny actually resounds with the concept of "complementarity," which is one of the most problematic modern *patriarchal* readings of biblical gender, especially regarding the creation accounts in Genesis. Ken Stone's queer reading of the Genesis myth is a direct attack on such a "gender complementarity" reading of the myth, which is frequently not only a thin veneer for the premise that women's place in society is to complement men, but also leaves any gender non-conforming subjects completely outside the scheme.[19] It is, of course, hardly helpful that Martin brings out, in this already complicated colonial project, an orientalizing sounding and appropriative fantasy in which Paul can be read as advocating that "the male would be the yin of the female yang."[20]

## Daniel Boyarin's *Gender*

*Gender* by Daniel Boyarin, which was published in Mark C. Taylor's methodological handbook *Critical Terms for Religious Studies*, occupies an intriguing place amongst the three examples addressed in this essay, and thus was intentionally left for the end. In this study, the we–they rhetoric functions underneath the surface of an otherwise impressive attempt of demonstrating the *similarities* between antiquity and modernity.

Boyarin argues that the split between two brands of feminism, represented by Monique Wittig and Luce Irigaray respectively, reproduce an ancient parting of the ways between Hellenistic Christianity and Rabbinical Judaism. The latter was fully committed to a naturalized conception of sex, thus affirming femininity (albeit, of course, only within its proper limits and expressions); the former promised transcendence which can nevertheless be only purchased by the effacement of femininity. Boyarin then proceeds to evaluate how such effacement was actually effected in antiquity:

> On my reading, then, these Christian imaginings of gender bending don't even really comprehend a "destabilization of gender identity." Rather, insofar as they are completely immured in the dualism of the flesh and the spirit, they represent no change whatsoever in the status of gender. All of these texts are mythic or ritual enactments of the "myth of the primal androgyne," and as such simply reinstate the metaphysics of substance, the split between Universal Mind and Disavowed Body which constitutes a reinstatement of masculinism: The androgyne in question always turns out somehow to be a male androgyne.[21]

While at this point this may seem to be a typical we–they approach to the ancient Mediterranean culture which is not able to comprehend a possible destabilization of

---

Laqueur 2003, 306: "no particular scientific view of difference necessarily favors one view of the place of women over another."

19 Cf. Stone 2006, esp. 52-53 and 63.

20 Martin 2006, 89.

21 Boyarin 1998, 126.

gender, it is the implied "as opposed to" that is especially surprising. It seems that as far as feminist thought goes, we are entrapped in the very same point. Thus, argues Boyarin, "in [Monique] Wittig's writing, not being a lesbian, that is, 'being a woman' seems finally as pejorative as it was in Philo and patristic writings."[22] This is certainly true: Wittig even argues that "woman" cannot be redeemed in the same way that we cannot redeem "slave" or the n-word.[23] Yet this hasty comparison occludes an important difference. For Philo and the (proto-orthodox) Church fathers, the existence of gender is – for better and worse – divinely mandated either as a result of a deserved fall or as a second-best bodily condition.[24] For Wittig, "woman" is a deceptive human cultural construct made by "men" in order to dominate and take advantage of those so designated. Thus, Wittig's call for the destruction of femininity can hardly be seen as a "reinstatement of masculinism." It can only be seen as such from the perspective of that very masculinism that assumes that gender *and* sex are already there, and waiting to be evaluated by the critic. But that would be accepting a premise that negates the very possibility of such criticism.[25]

Interesting as this may be for its own sake, let us try to return to the peculiar way the we–they paradigm is here employed. On the face of it, it is simple. Antiquity is not able to rise to the level of the modern Western subject, and thus its "gender bending" is only a "reinstatement of masculinism." But then Boyarin surprises us: one of the most important representatives of Western feminism cannot reach these heights either, and inadvertently falls into this same trap. But then, who does not? Who are the "we" implied in this comparison? Apparently, it is precisely the Western patriarchal establishment that Wittig attempts to dismantle. This establishment's is the only perspective from which one could premise sexual dimorphism, and it renders well-nigh impossible any attempts to cleverly overcome it.[26] Ostensibly, both Wittig and Hellenistic Christian writers were unable to see the fault inherent in their attempts at transcendence. Surprisingly (or perhaps not so much), rabbinical Judaism (and its modern representative Luce Irigaray) were closer to the truth in affirming sexual difference as such.[27] Yet this move to address the similarities between antiquity and modernity comes at a price. It uses the colonizing of antiquity in order to colonize and neutralize one of the main challenges

22 Boyarin 1998, 127.

23 Cf. Wittig 1992, 29-30.

24 Boyarin is of course well aware of this, and notes that it goes back to Philo of Alexandria: cf. Boyarin 1998, 120-121.

25 For discussion of this phenomenon in more detail as it pertains to modern readings of Gnosticism and critical theories (feminist included), see Cahana-Blum 2018, 98-105.

26 Such discourse has been incisively described by Lee Edelman as "terms that impose as ideological limit on political discourse as such, preserving in the process of absolute privilege of heteronormativity by rendering unthinkable, by casting outside the political domain, the possibility of a queer resistance to this organizing principle of communal relations" (Edelman 2004, 2).

27 Although, of course, in distinction to Irigaray, rabbinical Judaism used that difference oppressively towards women by limiting their role within society to that intimately connected with their bodies: Boyarin 1998, 131-132.

to Western ideological premises voiced by Wittig and her third-wave feminist followers such as Judith Butler. It colonizes modern feminist critique by occluding the crucial difference of a premise that is not accepted by Wittig but is accepted by proto-orthodox Christians: that sex is somehow divinely ordained. And it colonizes antiquity by not addressing other Christians, who did not accept this premise either. Gnostic Christians did not believe that sex or gender are divinely ordained, but saw them as an evil deceptive construct that originated in a malevolent entity that cannot be properly thought of as divine; in this, they came quite close to what Wittig would propound almost 2000 years later.[28] Thus, although Boyarin's project appears to be one of appeasement between modernity and antiquity, and bringing one to be read in the light of the other, under the surface the same colonial we–they approach is functioning. And, as we have seen, this approach is destined to lead to both distortion of antiquity, and the advancement of modern colonial stratagems.

## Conclusion

In this essay, I have detailed three examples a we–they paradigm being applied to antiquity, and the pitfalls such an approach introduces into scholarship. While comparison as such is an invaluable tool in the study of sexuality, and our awareness of difference is crucial, one needs to beware of embodying an ideal Western subject that looks down on Mediterranean primitives and their limited consciousness. Such an approach both advances the uncritical acceptance of Western modernity's colonial claims about itself, and precludes a nuanced understanding of antiquity. In Halperin's *One Hundred Years of Homosexuality*, this causes no distortion in our understanding of antiquity, but uncritically supports and advances harmful Western colonial concepts. In Martin's *The Queer History of Galatians 3:28*, on the other hand, this approach mostly distorts our understanding of the ancient sources. In Boyarin's *Gender*, both sides of the comparison suffer. Notwithstanding, all three studies make persuasive and pertinent points, and will undoubtably continue to be crucial to our understanding of ancient sexuality. Our awareness of the we–they paradigm they employ, however, will allow us to use their findings constructively, without their colonial baggage, which, now as then, has done very little to advance our understanding of ourselves or those who are not us.

28 There is, of course, an important difference between a cultural construct and superhuman malevolent personal entity, even if the implications of both are highly similar. For further discussion of the many parallels between Christian Gnosticism and radical feminism, Wittig included, see Cahana 2016.

# MYTHS AS 'CULTURAL VECTORS'

## Some reflections on Ancient Greece and Modern Ethnographic Traditions

**ABSTRACT** *This paper examines some aspects of the nature, function, and mode of operation of myths in ancient Greece in comparison with other cultures. In particular, I use Bronislaw Malinowski's studies of myths in the Trobriand Islands in order to highlight some aspects of Greek narratives about gods and heroes, and to stress the importance of a "constructive comparativism" for scholars of ancient Greek culture.*

In an outstanding pamphlet, M. Detienne – a Hellenist, historian of religions, anthropologist, and ethnologist – defends, with strength of purpose and *vis polemica*, the need for a "comparatisme constructif" in research on Ancient and Modern culture: scholars, encouraged to leave ivory towers of self-referentiality ("le 'chez-moi' … pour affirmer la spécificité d'une culture à l'originalité sans partage"), of Nationalisms ("on peut comparer que ce qui est comparable"), and of cultural value judgments (West *vs* East; primitive *vs* civilized), should choose as field of practice and experimentation the set of cultural representations between the societies of the past, the most distant and the closest, and the living human groups observed on the planet, yesterday or today.[1]

This statement belongs to a manifesto, both challenging and indispensable, which is part of an expanding field of study.[2] In this small but rich book, there is food for theoretical thought and for concrete operations for scholars of Ancient Greece and Rome, as well as Modern Africa, Italy, France or Great Britain, "qui ne visent nullement à établir des typologies non plus qu'à dresser des morphologies".[3] Among the many virtues of this "constructive and experimental comparativism" – and perhaps the most important – there is the possibility of putting "à distance de soi" and therefore understanding "comme naissent et grandissent les mythidéologies incrustées dans leur incomparabilité," in most cultural areas.[4]

Among these "mythidéologies," in an etymological wordplay that is both deliberate and meaningful, a special place is occupied by the "ideologies on myths", a field of study for classicists – especially Hellenists – and historians, anthropologists, and ethnologists.[5]

1 Detienne 2009, 44; cf. etiam: "le comparatiste qui veut construire ses objets doit pouvoir se déplacer sans passeport".

2 Cf., e.g., Detienne 2005; Calame and Lincoln 2012; Pébarthe 2016.

3 Detienne 2009, 11.

4 Detienne 2009, 173.

5 Cf. Malinowski 1926, 76 f.: "The science of mythology has been the meeting-point of various scholarships: the classical humanist …, the various tribes of archaeologists, … [the] historian and the sociologist, the student of literature, the grammarian, the Germanist and the Romanist, the

Now as then, an important, and not always moderate, dichotomy exists between those who study "Myth" in Ancient Greece and those who study myths in other modern ethnographical societies. What is more significant, among scholars of different aspects of the Ancient Greek world, such as philologists and historians of religions, there is no consensus about the study of myths.[6] Generally, but with some exceptions, these scholars often do not all work in a common direction – or, if they do not agree about topic or methodologies, they do not take advantage of diversity to expand their spectrum of studies; indeed, they challenge each other "to the sound of truths".[7]

The main goal of this paper is to contribute to the debate about myths in Ancient Greece using Detienne's method of "comparatisme constructif," exploring analogous narrative activities in other ethnographic modern societies, more or less far away from Greece. Through B.K. Malinoswki's studies on morphology, function, and mode of operation of traditional narratives in the Trobriand Islands, I will attempt to enable communication with and incentivize reflection on historical and philological research, in order to go beyond reification of textual tradition and the poetic-literary value, in the modern sense, of myths. These pages are thus intended to be a partial response to the invitation of those who, in the early twentieth century, encouraged the scholars of Ancient Greece to communicate with anthropologists and ethnologists, often to no avail.[8]

### Why Malinowski and the Greek Myths?

B. K. Malinowski (born Krakow 1884, died New Haven 1942) is considered the founding father of the modern British school of social anthropology.[9] He turned to anthropological and ethnographical studies after a PhD in philosophy (1908) at the University of Kra-

---

Celtic scholar and the Slavist ..., [the] logicians and [the] psychologists, ... the metaphysician and the epistemologist – to say nothing of such visitors as the theosophist, the modern astrologist, and the Christian Scientist, ... the psychoanalyst (...). So that when at last the poor anthropologist and student of folklore come to the feast, there are hardly any crumbs left for them!"

6 The first reify textual sources, as though they were the better documents useful to the reconstruction of certain cultural data; furthermore, they often scrutinize myths as though they were a poetic creation of individual minds, literary variations about a single theme. By contrast, some historians of religion consider myths as a universal category of mind, underestimating in some cases the differences between the cultural and social substratum of each historical society.

7 We can "appreciate" the nature of this intellectual dispute if we read, for example, Casadio 2009 and Calame 2011, 13 f. The French school of Gernet, Vernant, and Detienne and the Italian school of Pettazzoni and Brelich are distinctive in their wise comparativism, making use of other modern ethnographic cultures. For bibliography on different interpretations of myths cf., e.g., Jensen 2009; Dowden and Livingstone 2011.

8 Malinowski 1926, 77: "If I have conveyed an impression of chaos and confusion, if I have inspired a sinking feeling towards the incredible mythological controversy with all the dust and din which it raises, I have achieved exactly what I wanted. For I shall invite my readers to step outside the closed study of the theorist into the open air of the anthropological field, and to follow me in my mental flight back to the years which I spent among a Melanesian tribe of New Guinea."

9 On Malinowski, cf., e.g., Firth 1960b(?); Young 2004.

kow; the influence of various figures from his childhood, who in different ways instilled the passion in him, nurtured his ideas and contributed to defining his own theories. His father was a professor of Slavic Philology and studied Polish dialects and folklore; his mother travelled much with the young boy in the Mediterranean; and at the University of Krakow Malinowski read the *Golden Bough* of Sir J. Frazer, while at Leipzig he was influenced by the folk psychology of W. Wundt. He studied at the London School of Economics, where he taught in the Department of Sociology and obtained his DSc degree (1916), with two published works on the Australian Aborigines and on the Mailu.[10]

These latter works are the outcome of the research Malinowski conducted in Papua New Guinea, on a scholarship from the University of London and the London School of Economics. He traveled between Australia and Papua New Guinea from 1914 to 1918, carrying out fieldwork at Mailu Island and then, more famously, in the Trobriand Islands. In 1922 his book *Argonauts of the Western Pacific* was published, earning Malinowski instant and international fame. With the exception of some travel in Africa, after 1918 he lived in Europe and visited the United States (1926), teaching and conducting research on the populations of Arizona and Mexico.[11]

Malinowski's research interests were several and various: community laws, religion, social relations, kingship, magic, economics, poetry, and psychology. He also wrote about myth throughout his career.[12] In *Argonauts of the Western Pacific*, he dedicates a whole section to the "Mythology of the Kula", a ceremonial exchange system conducted in the Milne Bay Province of Papua New Guinea: myths are analysed in "sociological terms" for their normative function in the society, and as variants in a complex context of transformation.[13] In his outstanding essay "Ethnology and the Study of Society", Malinowski scrutinizes the pragmatic, material, and even biological conception of the nature of myth and culture at large, following the work of Durkheim and Mauss.[14] In two important papers, he examines in depth the relation between instinctive life (with its unconscious determinants of human behavior) and social institutions, through Freudian innovations in the field of psychology.[15] Malinowski's psychoanalytic interests culminated in his classic functionalist statement on myth from 1926, *Myth in Primitive Psychology*, where he recalls and elaborates on some elements from *Argonauts*. Other developments in his studies can be seen in two more essays, "Myth as Dramatic Development of Dogma" and "The Foundations of Faith and Morals".[16]

Throughout his life, Malinowski's work shows a remarkable continuity with subtle, but important, developments in the field of the study of myth.[17] There are, however,

10 Firth 1960a, 2 f.

11 Cf. Firth 1960a.

12 For a useful anthology with commentary cf. Strenski 1992.

13 Malinowski 1922.

14 Malinowski 1921.

15 Malinowski 1923; Idem 1927b; cf. Stocking 1986.

16 The first in an undated later essay, reprinted in Malinowski 1962a; for the second cf. Idem 1936.

17 Cf. Streski 1992, xi-xxxii.

certain enduring concepts that underpin his reflections throughout all of his anthropological research. In this context, some sections of the essay *Myth in Primitive Psychology* are particularly revealing, as Malinowski considers myths as documents of real life and as a heuristic category in order to understand the societies who used them.

There are several reasons for invoking Malinowski in a study of the morphology, function, and mode of operation of myths in Ancient Greece.[18] First of all, by experiencing the everyday life of his subjects along with them, the anthropologist recorded their stories live; he attended the performances and he could reconstruct and examine deeply their contextual elements. Hellenists cannot be present at a recitation of Homeric rhapsodies or of Pindaric epinician odes; we will never appreciate the dynamics of voices, sounds, perfumes, spaces, emotions, and interconnections between the narrator/actor and his audience during a ritual. Direct "participant observation" is, nevertheless, the best condition for understanding the most important aspects of a different culture.[19]

Second, Malinowski stresses the importance of cultural context in order to understand the nature and function of myths:

> For an observer, therefore, it is necessary to become fully acquainted with the social organization of the natives if he wants really to grasp its [i.e., the myth's] traditional aspect .... He will also clearly see that each of them [i.e., the myths] is only a part, and a rather significant one, of a much bigger story, which cannot be read except from native life.[20]

In other words, we need as much as possible to have a complete knowledge and awareness of the social organization and its everyday practices in order to understand the myths that society produced.

Third, Malinowski considers myths as part of the functional, pragmatic, or performed dimension of culture. For the anthropologist, myths are performative acts, like oaths, laws, and prayers, which are important not for what they are but for what they do. They operate practically and maintain the legitimacy of social arrangements, guide human behaviors and choices, and preserve the society as a whole: myth is thus a "hard-worked active force."[21]

Last but not least, Malinowski creates "sensitivity for the critical role of context in interpreting the meaning of myths"; he applies "the lesson of psychoanalysis to the study of culture"; he shows "exemplary conceptual self-awareness about the epistemological status of the category of myth."[22]

---

18 Cf. Strenski 1992, xi-xxvii; Strenski 1987.

19 For this concept, in general and with references to its limits, cf. DeWalt – DeWalt 2011.

20 Malinowski 1926, 93.

21 Idem, 79.

22 Strenski 1992, xxi-xxvii.

### What a myth can be and what it can do

The first important issue analysed by Malinowski is the nature of myth as ethnographic category; that is, as a hermeneutic instrument useful for distinguishing some particular types of stories that have social relevance. These narratives, which contain clear references to community life in all its aspects, allow the anthropologist to understand the reality of the populations who used them:

1. Myth as it exists in a savage community, that is, in its *living primitive form*, is not merely a story told but a reality lived. It is not of the nature of fiction, such as we read today in a novel, but it is a living reality, believed to have once happened in primeval times, and continuing ever since to influence the world and human destinies. This myth is to the savage what, to a fully believing Christian, is the Biblical story of Creation, of the Fall, of the Redemption by Christ's Sacrifice on the Cross. As our sacred story lives in our ritual, in our morality, as it governs our faith and controls our conduct, even so does his myth for the savage;[23]
2. Myth fulfils in *primitive culture* an indispensable function: it expresses, enhances, and codifies belief; it safeguards and enforces morality; it vouches for the efficiency of ritual and contains practical rules for the guidance of man. Myth is thus a vital ingredient of human civilization; it is not an idle tale, but a hard-worked active force; it is not an intellectual explanation or an artistic imagery, but a pragmatic charter of primitive faith and moral wisdom;[24]
3. Myth is above all a cultural force.[25]

Malinowski considers myths not as untrue stories told for entertainment, but as a "pragmatic charter of primitive faith and moral wisdom." Through the stories they tell, these narratives reveal the considerations of a certain population about relevant social questions in a distinctive historical situation. Each myth transfers to a faraway past and transfigures through "primitive" personages (e.g. animals) and places (e.g. caves) the origins of community and its norms, positions of power, and social relations. In this sense, myth is a piece of the mechanism of society performing its task in maintaining the social or cultural whole; furthermore, myths are not only basic explanations of reality, but active parts of culture, like commands or deeds.[26]

---

23 Malinowski 1926, 78. Unless I specify otherwise, the use of italics and underlining in citations from the works of Malinowski is mine.

24 Idem, 579.

25 Idem, 119.

26 Cf. Malinowski 1926, 87 f.: "Myth ... is not an intellectual reaction upon a puzzle, but an explicit act of faith, born from the innermost instinctive and emotional reaction to the most formidable and haunting idea. Nor are the stories about 'the origins of rites and customs' told in mere explanation of them. They never explain in any sense of the word: they always state a precedent which constitutes an ideal and a warrant for its continuance, and sometimes practical directions for the procedure. ... This definition would create an imaginary, non-existent class of narrative, the etiological myth, corresponding to a non-existent desire to explain, leading a futile existence

In modern studies of Greek culture there is, even now, a division in terms of analysis between historians of religion and scholars of philology and literature. The latter group tends to read textual sources (e.g. Homeric texts or tragedies) as 'poetry' in a modern and/or Romantic sense, that is, as outcomes of personal reflections and emotions, and it tightly ties them to writing.[27] These scholars thus risk underestimating and, in some cases, misunderstanding another value of the content of these sources, and their dynamic of composition in relation to social groups: they do not recognise the social and collective *substratum* that gave rise to these narratives, an aspect that has had more attention from historians of religion and anthropologists.[28]

Most of Malinowski's statements are valid for scholars of classics. In Ancient Greece, "telling myths" is a phenomenon that is always part of a wider civic and ritual context, whether public, such as an athletic competition or a procession for a god (occasions that the community, as a whole or in part, is actively involved in), or private, such as nurses telling stories to children.[29] This practice is an integral part of the system that Sourvinou-Inwood called "*polis* religion," in which religious and social practices are "interconnected." There is no private, personal relationship with the divine, nor does politics have a secular imprint;[30] on the contrary, the entire community participates collectively and according to specific roles in ritual practices, which are intended to sustain and update the values of the community itself.[31] In this "interconnected reality" telling myths might, for example, define tributes paid to the gods, recall the origins of the community, model patterns of social behavior, impose restrictive rules, define social relations and hierarchies, allow a sovereign to justify their territorial claims, or emphasize the ethnic identity of their community, referring to the heroic past.

By conveying information about the origins, traditions, and customs of a community, myths are part of what anthropologists call "patrimonio tradizionale," the "mémoire

as an 'intellectual effort', and remaining outside native culture and social organization with their pragmatic interests. … The intellectual nature of a story is exhausted with its text, but the functional, cultural, and pragmatic aspect of any native tale is manifested as much in its enactment, embodiment, and contextual relations as in the text."

27 Some aspects of such an interpretation can be found in recent studies of narratology on Homer (e.g. de Jong 2001). While this approach reveals Homeric poems as architectural structures that are well-balanced in its parts, it risks ignoring other structural aspects of the poems, such as their oral gestation and crystallization into writing, their stratification and social function, and the aesthetic of mythical narratives, which makes them extremely different as a cultural product from modern poetry. For this concept cf. Rossi 1989; Gentili 2006.

28 On the social relevance of myths cf. López Eire and Velasco López 2012.

29 On the context of myths cf. Buxton 1994; regarding literary genres, Woodard 2007, 19-254; Dowden and Livingstone 2011, 109-207.

30 On the 'interconnected' nature of Greek cosmology cf. Oudemans and Lardinois 1987, 82-106.

31 Cf. Sourvinou-Inwood 1988; Idem 1990, 295-322. For a revision of this category cf. J. Kindt 2012. Giordano (2005, 347 s.; 2006, 53-74) speaks, adequately, of "civic religion," "in the sense that the municipal, local dimension saturates all its spheres: the gods were one with their polis and its citizens, politai."

collective" of Halbwachs; the most recent cultural studies translate this into "cultural memory," which has distinctive and ethnic functions as regards identity.[32]

Another concept analysed by Malinowski and highly evident in Greek culture is the "epichoric" nature of myth; that is, the deep link between myths and the community which, from generation to generation, tells them. No myth is a universal story, valid for all communities, but it is functional *in primis*, and almost exclusively, for the territory that uses it. Greek language is very clear in this sense: τά ἐπιχώρια, often in conjunction with the genitive of a given city or population, is the set of traditions that constitute the authoritative past of the center itself;[33] οἱ ἐπιχώριοι are the indigenous custodians or interpreters of these traditions;[34] gods and heroes are ἐπιχώριοι.[35] Every community therefore has its cults and traditions, which are ἐπιχώρια (i.e., related to a single χώρα), first as opposed to other communities, equipped with different traditions. The opposition between the different traditions is thus functional both for the "internal" mythical foundation of each community, and for the distinction in terms of ethnic identity from "external" communities.[36]

#### How myths arise, change, and keep themselves up to date

Another relevant feature of myths Malinowski stresses is their variable nature. Myths are not unaltered narratives; they accommodate themselves to different historical situations, such as social changes:

> [Myth] is ... <u>constantly regenerated</u>; every historical change creates its mythology, which is, however, but indirectly related to historical fact.[37] ... One of the most interesting phenomena connected with traditional precedent and charter is <u>the adjustment of myth and mythological principle</u> to cases in which the very foundation of such mythology is fragrantly violated ... The result is that there come(s) into existence a special class of mythological stories which justify and account for the anomalous state of affairs.[38]

---

32 Cf., e.g., Halbwachs 1950; Assmann 1988, 9-19; Idem 1992; 2006. For studies of 'cultural memory' and ethnic identity in Ancient Greece cf. Proietti 2012. On memory more generally as cultural instrument cf. Erll and Nünning 2008; Erll 2011.

33 Cf., e.g., Paus. 10. 15, 5; etiam ἐπιχώριον ἐστὶ / κατ τὸ ἐπιχώριον: Paus. 1. 23, 4; 3. 26, 7; 4. 7, 9.

34 Cf., e.g., Paus. 2. 11, 5; 4. 35, 9; 6. 6, 4 (cf. λόγος δὲ τῶν ἐπιχωρίων: Paus. 7. 23, 1; ὁ τῶν ἐπιχωρίων ἐξηγητής: e.g. Paus. 1. 13, 8; 7. 6, 5; 9. 3, 3).

35 For gods cf., e.g., Paus. 1. 21, 6; 3. 26, 1; for heroes cf. Paus. 4. 33, 6; 5. 13, 8; 10. 1, 10. In general cf. Pirenne-Delforge 2008, 244-248.

36 Cf. Müller 1991, 50; Graf 2011, 211 et passim.

37 Malinowski 1926, 122.

38 Idem, 94 f.

Most of the sources from Ancient Greece confirm this statement.[39] The function of myths as cultural vectors is guaranteed by their own formal structure. Myths have a natural predisposition to variation in the form of updating and re-contextualization. These narratives are not immutable; that is, they are not given once and for all to a community.[40] Instead, they manifest themselves in a large number of versions: along with a "diachoric" variety, linked to the specificities of communities on a geographical level (Athens, Sparta, and Argos each had their mythical heritage), there is also a "diachronic" variety, linked to the evolution of traditional heritage across time in the same historical community (such as Tegea in the Archaic or Hellenistic age), or of the communities in relation to each other. The multiple versions of a story can be defined as variants only if this term does not bring with it the logic of direct derivation (vertically, a version generates another) and/or progressive impoverishment (the more ancient the original version, the more subsequent ones are more or less faithful imitations).[41] There is no hierarchy of importance between the versions, but only the "diachrony" of a before and an after that are related to structural evolution and chronological change.

As part of collective memory, mythical stories operate on the model of "invention of tradition," developed by English anthropology.[42] From transmitted heritage, the Greek community, through specific individuals (singers, politicians, philosophers etc.), who can be called "factors of agentivity," or, from another point of view, "guardians of tradition," create new stories adapted to the circumstances, in order to strengthen, expand or upgrade cultural and social patrimony. The act of creation is authoritative when it draws on an existing property, which is the antecedent; it is also innovative because it extends the antecedent, helping to provide new material for further creations. This does not imply the non-veracity of the story itself. In the oral traditional societies creation is an inspired "sacred" act, as shown in epic poetry, and true, because the creator is the mouthpiece of a tangible reality that all the community recognizes and respects.[43]

The myths, as evidenced by the etymology of some of the Greek words for them (ὁ μῦθος, τὸ ἔπος, ὁ λόγος etc.), are linked to verbal narration, to listening and viewing: actions with strong pragmatic value that are carried out on specific occasions.[44] Each myth is productive first for the community in which it exists, and is transmitted or performed in the rites. At the same time, however, the myths travel through the bards, the lyric poets, the vases, and above all through the memory of those who, by moving, change community in order to be present at the ritual practices of other communities

39 Cf. infra the examples about Orestes myths.

40 Cf. Vernant 1981; Zaidman and Schmitt-Pantel 1992, 3-18; Schirripa 2010, 12-14; Parker 2011, 1-39.

41 Giordano 2004, 184: "[un mito è una] variante che si situa nella costellazione di varianti preesistenti sull'asse temporale, e contemporanee sull'asse spaziale."

42 Cf. Hobsbawm and Range 1983.

43 Cf. Veyne 1984; Calame 2015, 16 f. On the power of mythical narrative cf. Lincoln 1989. On mythos-logos cf., e.g., Buxton 1999; Fowler 2011; Hawes 2014a. Cf. Malinowski 1926, 102: "It [i.e., Myth] is to a native neither a fictitious story, nor an account of a dead past; it is a statement of a bigger reality still partially alive."

44 Cf., e.g., Lincoln 1999, 3-18; Calame 2015, 15 f.

(e.g. the Great Dionysia, where spectators flocked from all over Greece), promoting an osmotic process of transmission from one space to another, which is equivalent to a new contextualization of mythical material in a new civic horizon.

By way of example of the variety of Greek myths in time and space ("them") and of the limits of some modern interpretations ("we"), we can evoke the copious traditions on the matricide Orestes, from Homer to Aeschylus.[45] In the *Odyssey*, where there is no reference to the contamination (μίασμα), purification (κάθαρσις), or process of the hero at the Areopagus of Athens, Orestes avenges his father, by killing Aegisthus and probably his mother Clytemnestra, although this last act is only covertly mentioned in the poem.[46] No reference is made to a hero's punishment for the sin he committed; Orestes restores in a right and honorable manner the order that came down with the violent death of Agamemnon at the hands of Aegisthus.[47]

When, from the seventh century BC at least and for the Archaic and Classical periods, new laws are adopted for the treatment of murderers (e.g. the Dracon law, *IG* I³ 104), the types of crimes and of tribunals (δίκη φόνου at Athens), and the processes of contamination and purification (e.g. *Lex sacra* of Selinous, *SEG* XLIII 630), new myths are created about Orestes' contamination, purification, and punishment through, for example, the narrative segments of the persecution by the Erinyes or the ritual purification in Arcadia or at Keryneia.[48] Although some of these traditions may be later than 458 BC and they may echo some aspects of the Athenian version, they are all epichoric traditions about the hero, linked to a historical moment and a very precise geographic and religious space, which cannot always be reconstructed *in toto*.[49] The *Oresteia* of Aeschylus finds its significance within a horizon of Athenian traditions in the fifth century BC; only later, because of the transmission process, has it become, perilously, *la version par excellence* for us today.

---

45 For the ancient sources cf. Lesky 1939. The prevailing approach in existing studies is a classical-centrist analysis that treats the story of the hero's judicial trial at the Athenian Areopagus, as staged by Aeschylus in 458 BC, as the version par excellence of the myth of Orestes; by taking this as the starting point, earlier mythical accounts, or versions set somewhere other than Argos/ Mycenae or Athens (e.g. the versions attested by Homer, Pindaric poetry, and Herodotus), are usually interpreted as preparatory stages for the Aeschylean exploit, while later ones are read as more or less successful reproductions of the tragic model, forming the descending arc of this hero's mythic parabola in the Greek world. The most extreme example of this kind of approach is Defradas 1954. For an overview of these studies and the often opposed interpretations cf. Pucci 2017.

46 For the killing of Aegisthus cf., e.g., Hom. Od. 1. 28 s.; for the matricide cf. Hom. Od. 3. 303-310.

47 Cf., e.g., Hom. Od. 1. 35-47; 298-302.

48 For the first mention of Erinyes cf. Stesich. fr. 181a, ll. 14-24; for the purification in Arcadia cf., e.g., Paus. 8. 34, 1-4; for the rituals at Keryneia cf. Paus.7. 25, 7; schol. Soph. Oed. Col. 42.

49 For obvious reasons, this statement does not intend to deny the relationship between the attested traditions, because, as we have seen, mythical narratives arise from an antecedent that acts as a basic element. However, this does not mean that the more recent traditions are imagined as mechanical copies of the preceding ones.

The birth of new traditions does not imply that the versions without the purification of the hero present in Homer disappeared or became irrelevant over time for other performance contexts. For example, in *Pythian* 11 (most probably 474 BC) Pindar recounts, in the same manner as Homer, the hero's revenge without referring to persecutor Erinyes or purification rites, and he set these events at Amyclai, in Laconia.[50] Sophocles, in his *Electra* (maybe after 416 BC), staged, in the same Aeschylean Athens, a similar version in which Orestes revenges his father and kills his mother, with no trial.

By reading the mythical traditions about Orestes both from a diachronic perspective, across the evolution of the laws of blood crime and of purification in Greek religions, and a diachoric one, through the structural differences among multiple communities, it is possible to interpret these traditions not as literary variations on revenge within epic, lyric, and tragedy, but as mythical, that is, social, religious, and cultural narrative patterns linked to specific celebrations (Great Dionysia, Pythian games etc.) or periodical rituals in specific communities. So, by these myths modern scholars can reconstruct several aspects of the social life of the various Ancient Greek communities at specific historical moments.

## Orality *vs* literacy

One of Malinowski's most interesting remarks about myth concerns the effects of the dichotomy between orality and literacy in the creation and transformation of myths over time. This is a debated question that has not yet found a satisfactory solution.[51] The anthropologist offers a key interpretation of the static and limited nature of our textual testimonies and the dynamic, concrete, and tangible reality of cultural and mythical traditions in context:

> The limitation of the study of myth to the mere examination of texts has been fatal to a proper understanding of its nature. The forms of myth which come to us from classical antiquity and from the ancient sacred books of the East and other similar sources have come down to us without the context of living faith, without the possibility of obtaining comments from true believers, without the concomitant knowledge of their social organization, their practised morals, and their popular customs – at least without the full information which the modern field-worker can easily obtain. Moreover, there is no doubt that in their present literary form these tales have suffered a very considerable transformation at the hands of scribes, commentators, learned priests, and theologians. It is necessary to go back to primitive mythology in order to learn the secret of its life in the study

50 Pind. Pyth. 11. 15-37; cf. also Pind. Nem. 11. 33-38.

51 On orality vs literacy in Ancient Greece on a general level cf., e.g., Thomas 1989; Eadem 1992; Rossi 1992, 77-106. On this dichotomy in relation to Greek myths cf. Morgan 2000, 24-30 (with particular focus on the birth of philosophical thought) and Hawes 2014b.

of myth which is still alive – before, mummified in priestly wisdom, it has been enshrined in the indestructible but lifeless repository of dead religions.[52]

It is clear and indisputable from the sources: our knowledge of myths and rituals in Ancient Greece is doubly limited. It is secondhand, based on written works that have set a cultural fact, otherwise dynamic, in a closed form together with a static view; it is partial because these same sources have crystallized and passed down specific versions, tied to particular moments of performance, at the risk of producing in the modern reader the illusion that they are the only ones. The *Iliad* and the *Odyssey*, as demonstrated by various studies on orality, are only two of many detailed forms that the stories about the Trojan War and the return of Odysseus have taken.[53]

In examining mythical tales in a given community it is therefore necessary to keep in mind two levels: that of occasional or repeated performance, verbal-factual and circumstantial in time and space, for us often lost; and transmission across time, entrusted to writing, which provides a vision of those myths that is often layered, confusing, and incomplete. In general, archaeological and epigraphic evidence is most important in reconstructing ritual context and some aspects of content; textual documentation by contrast allows us to integrate this data with the narration of what happened on site, why and how at any given time. Nevertheless, all the apparatus of sounds, sights, and smells of the performative occasion is lost, no matter how powerful the imagination of the modern spectator of an ancient reality.

In order to read textual sources, it is necessary to consider some specific data. As argued effectively by Ercolani, the Greek culture of the Archaic and Classical periods feeds on "texts" in the sense of "any elaboration (oral and/or written) of a message destined for an audience (i.e. intended for an addressee)," and "circumstances," that is "any social event of collective import."[54] The connection between the two realities – texts and circumstances – is carried out at multiple levels (material and type of song, specific references to the community context, etc.), and it explains the complexity of the Greek poetic phenomenon as a "real experience."[55]

Progressively, according to the diachronic evolution of Greek civilization, from oral/aural societies to cultures of writing in the Classical and Hellenistic periods, myths are put in writing, catalogued, and organized into genealogies through the works, written, of historiography, erudition and mythography. The transition from oral to written forms is nodal for the fate of myths over time, and it can be considered, in an analytical key, one of the founding acts of "mythology," understood as a collection of all myths according to a precise chronological order.[56]

---

52 Malinowski 1926, 78 f.

53 For orality in Homeric studies cf., e.g., Montanari, Rengakos, and Tsagalis 2012; Bierl 2015.

54 Ercolani 2014, 14.

55 Palmisciano 2014, 19: "There was concreteness in the experience of poetry, even tangibility."

56 Cf. Fowler 2006; Idem 2016. In light of these observations, we can understand and appreciate

By way of example of the limits of our textual documentation and of the related interpretative risks, it is possible to cite the case of the purification of Orestes at Troezen, accomplished, perhaps in two distinct moments, on the stone (λίθος) of Artemis Λυκεία and in the booth (σκηνή) of Apollo Θεάριος.[57] Pausanias' testimony is synthetic and unique, and it does not allow us to understand fully the dynamics of the story, the typology of purifiers and the function of the objects used. Modern scholars, struggling to reconstruct the narrative, have therefore invoked comparisons with other traditions, supposedly as precedents, such as the purification of Apollo at Tempe, the trial of Orestes at the Areopagus at Athens, and the supplication of the hero at Artemis' shrine in Arcadia.[58]

Many of the reconstructions proposed by scholars, based on written testimonies and on comparisons with other traditions, always written, run into two problems: on the specific plane of Pausanias' testimony, they deprive the epichoric version of its contextual value, while on the general level of the hermeneutic of myths, they reduce the overall interpretation of the various traditions to the creation of a *stemma codicum* of versions *recentiores* and more or less *deteriores*. The testimony of the tradition at Troezen must be interpreted as the crystallized residue of oral and maybe written traditions stratified over time and submerged in the processes of transmission. However, it had to be well rooted in the territory of Troezen, and well linked, first and foremost, to the political, social, and religious structure of the community.

The tradition of Orestes' purification lived in the cultural patrimony of Troezen as a piece of the community's identity and an example of norms and ritual practices. Only later, and for modern scholars, who could not observe a rite on the *agorà* of the city, did it become a decontextualized, static story, which is marked in the chronological succession of before and after, and which has lost the concreteness of the simultaneity

---

what Malinowski (1926, 119) wrote about the origins of literary genres: "Myth contains germs of the future epic, romance, and tragedy."

57 Paus. 2. 31, 4; 31, 8-9. In the case of the stone in front of the sanctuary of Artemis, we read that nine men of the city of Troezen (ἄνδρες Τροιζηνίων ἐννέα) in a distant mythical past (ποτέ) set Orestes there (ἐφ' οὗ) to purify him (ἐκάθηραν) after his matricide. In the case of the booth, we read that the hero had been lodged there, far from all others, to eat and be purified (καθίσαντες δὲ ἐνταῦθα ἐκάθαιρον καὶ εἱστίων, ἐς ὃ ἀφήγνισαν), since upon his arrival none of the inhabitants of the place wished to receive him in their own home because of the stain of matricide (πρὶν γρ ἐπὶ τῷ αἵματι καθαρθῆναι τῆς μητρός, Τροιζηνίων οὐδεὶς πρότερον ἤθελεν αὐτὸν οἴκῳ δέξασθαι). After a brief reference to the bay tree that grew from the instruments used for the purification and buried in front of the temple of Apollo, Pausanias mentions that Orestes was purified by many means (καθαρσίοις ἄλλοις), including water from the Hippocrene (ὕδατι τῷ ἀπὸ τῆς Ἵππου κρήνης).

58 Cf., e.g., Mele 2011, 361: "[the myth of purification of Oreste at Troezen is] manifestamente … una costruzione ad maiorem gloriam di Trezene, trasformata, come nelle abitudini locali, in un punto di confluenza di quanti più miti possibili [e.g. that of Pherekyd. FGrHist 3 F 135], poco rispettosa del modello [i.e., the purification of Apollo at Tempe]." For the complete sources and other interpretations cf. Pucci 2016.

and the depth of the succession of the events. If this is so, it is necessary to map other channels of transmission such as iconography or epigraphy, in order to accomplish a more complete and emic perception and vision of ancient cultural data.

## Myths *vs* history and geography

A last interesting observation by Malinowski concerns the link between real history and stories told in myths. He writes:

> As far as the sociological theory of these legends goes the historical reconstruction is irrelevant. … The historical consideration of myth is interesting, therefore, in that it shows that myth, taken as a whole, cannot be sober dispassionate history, since it is always made ad hoc to fulfil a certain sociological function, to glorify a certain group, or to justify an anomalous status. These considerations show us also that to the native mind immediate history, semi-historic legend, and unmixed myth flow into one another, from a continuous sequence, and fulfil really the same sociological function.[59]

The question of the historicity of myths is ancient, and bibliography about this topic is as extensive as it is full of contention.[60] In each myth, there are several references to the real life of a community, in terms both of geography and of historical events; nevertheless, the stories transfigure their references on a mythical level, often making them implicit or tacit. As an example, in Ancient Greece, mythical stories are set at historic sites, such as Argos, Sparta, or Megalopolis. Often the places which serve as mythical locations coincide with the communities where songs or rituals are performed. Nevertheless, narrative setting and geographical ritual space do not always coincide. In any case, it is important to recall Korzybski's statement that "the map is not the territory"; that is, we should not mechanically confuse the model of reality provided by myths with reality itself, in the case of an Argive myth for an Argive community, nor in that of a laconic story for a Theban community.[61]

We can turn again to Orestes. Several traditions are attested around the foundation of a center by the hero, Ὀρέστειον, in Arcadia. The sources are discordant and, at least from Euripides, it seems there was more than one Ὀρέστειον in the region.[62] It is true that in real geography the centers identified in the sources did not correspond to the centers as they existed concretely. However, although it is true that the map does not correspond to the territory, it is equally true that in the collective memory all sites identified as Ὀρέστειον existed on a mythical level as places of worship.

59 Malinowski 1926, 102.

60 Cf., e.g., Brillante 1990; Assmann 2006.

61 Korzybski 1933.

62 E.g. Pherekyd. FGrHist 3 F 135; Eur. Or. 1643-1647; Eur. El. 1273-1275. For other sources and modern interpretations cf. Pucci 2017, 257-269.

## Conclusion

By way of conclusion, we can affirm that Malinowski's reflections on myths in Papua New Guinea are significant for modern scholars of Ancient Greek culture. In general, mythical events allow us, both modern scholars and passionates of classical world, to reflect on socially relevant issues, such as the maintenance of order, the origins of the cosmos, behavior in war, or the treatment of killers. As communities change, including in their relationships with other *poleis*, they encounter new problems, and new economic, trade, and cultural considerations; social practices must adapt. Myths, which are carriers of these practices and social and religious norms, also register these changes.[63]

A traditional story, that is, a myth, can be imagined as a basic narrative link between, for example, the name of a character and a distinctive feature: Orestes and paternal revenge, or Oedipus and incest and parricide. Such a narrative grows in time and space according to the socio-historical and geographical contingencies of the community in which myths are performed. The basic link between Orestes and revenge or Oedipus and incest expands to include the "purification" event when the Greek community begins to experience family revenge as a difficult problem to solve; the notion of contamination is necessary to the efficacy of cathartic rites.

According to this principle, which we can call 'epichoric contextualization,' each mythical tradition must be analyzed in the light of the spaces in which it is attested and for which it is designed, as well as the historical moment of each source; where possible, we must seek a reference point and trace evolutionary paths over time. It is also necessary at least to search for possible links in similar traditions, whether diachronically or synchronically connected with those contexts. Myths are multi-purpose and, as such, the same image cannot have the same function in two different places.[64]

As Malinowski wrote,

> myth is, therefore, an indispensable ingredient of all culture. It is … constantly regenerated; every historical change creates its mythology, which is, however, but indirectly related to historical fact. Myth is a constant by product of living faith, which is in need of miracles; of sociological status, which demands precedent; of moral rule, which requires sanction. … Folk-tales, legends, and myths must

63 See Iliad XXIV. Regarding the treatment of the corpse by the victorious in the battle. If in the first twenty-three books of the poem, the act of destruction of the dead body? (ἀεικίζειν) is customary rule, linked to the honor of the victorious?, in the last part, through the intervention of Zeus, Achilles has to return Hector's corpse to father Priam. By changing the mythical story, the poem records the change within the Panhellenic norm; cf. Cerri 1986.

64 Gernet 2004, 15, 48 s. et passim. Lincoln 1999: 150 s.: "Ideally, one would like to study each variant not only in its relation to all other variants, but also with attention to the social and historic situation in which each variant made its appearance and found its appearance and found its reception, so that one could get a sense of how interplay between narrators and audience produced narrative innovations, taxonomic modifications, and consequent shifts in the distribution of advantages over the course of time. To put it differently, our task is not finished until we have considered texts, contexts, intertexts, pretexts, subtexts, and consequences"

be lifted from their flat existence on paper, and places in the three-dimensional reality of full life.[65]

If the anthropologist, according to Malinowski, "must relinquish their comfortable position in the chaise longue on the veranda of the missionary compound ..., he must go out into the villages,"[66] it would be desirable for modern scholars of Ancient Greek culture to relinquish their comfortable position in the ivory tower of philology and Hellenic-centrism, and to compare Hellenic culture with other cultures, in order to try to understand what has been irremediably lost from Ancient Greece.

Such an approach would have multiple benefits:

1. beyond philological research, which is necessary and basic, the interpretation of myths as social documents would allow us to appreciate the cultural potential of these ancient narratives for reconstructing aspects of the political, religious, and cultural life of the Greeks; thus it is possible to show the similarities and the differences between "we" and "them," beyond the grounded statement that modern European thought derives *recta via* from Ancient Greece;[67]
2. since the written texts are testimonies, partial and crystallized, of a dynamic reality made not only of words, the study of Ancient Greek culture would benefit from a more correct distinction between "transmitted" and "not transmitted," that is, submerged, and between what is "relevant" and "not relevant" on the interpretative level, in order to attribute to all the testimonies a fairer value, beyond the selections made since antiquity among cultural data;[68] this affirmation is even more significant, because what is "relevant" to us in social life is not said to be the same for the Ancient Greeks and *vice versa*;
3. furthermore, modern scholars would look differently at the question of the veracity of mythical tales, rightly acknowledged in their social and cultural validity for the communities that guarded them; they would give a different weight to the modern social practice of storytelling in order to understand reality and to renew or modify it – how else would we explain the use of stories today, told to children or indeed to adults?[69]
4. myths allow modern scholars to confront cultural and conceptual realities other than their own, which cannot be harnessed in their interpretative cultural schemes;

---

65 Malinowski 1926, 122.

66 Ibid., 123.

67 On the Ancient Greek roots of modern Europe and on a more prominent reading of Western identity cf. Bettini 2016.

68 By way of example, we can cite the Romantic and Idealistic approach to Ancient Greek tragedy, considered the manifestation of an Ancient Greek spirit that never existed before (e.g. Hegel, Nietzsche); cf., e.g., Billings 2014.

69 In this sense, we can speak of myths as a universal phenomenon, which escapes, in form but perhaps not in content, the time and space in which it manifests itself.

scholars are thus invited to think in Ancient Greek terms about Ancient Greek culture (Ἕλληνες ἐξ Ἑλλήνων σαφηνίζειν);

5. at the same time, the comparison between Ancient Greek and modern ethnographic societies allows us to see new interpretive paths, but, above all, to limit the damage of a dominant "Hellenic-centrism", as well as of "modernism"; comparative studies show the relativity of the previously quoted Ancient Greek proverb in relation to ancient testimonies, and the importance of pluralistic research in reflecting more productively on the category of myth.

## Acknowledgements

I wish to thank Karmen MacKendrick and Jonathan Cahana-Blum for giving me the opportunity to publish this contribution, the proofreaders for their valuable recommendations, and, last but not least, Manuela Giordano for his expansive and untiring discussions with me about myths in Ancient Greece.

# LIBERATING LEVI

## A Cultural-Evolutionary Approach to Aramaic and Greek Levi Beyond Denominational Essentialism

JESSICA VAN 'T WESTEINDE

**ABSTRACT** *Post-Enlightenment and particularly nineteenth-century scholarship has been immensely influenced by categorical and binary thinking, a mode that was shaped by the identity politics of the period. This has skewed our perspective on ancient texts and material. A particularly strong and persistent urge to dichotomize is often present when there is a question of what is perceived as 'Jewish'/'Judaism,' versus 'Christian'/'Christianity'. As a matter of fact, even our definition of religion problematizes our interpretation of ancient expressions of 'religious' experience, identity, or affiliation. Taking into account Michael Satlow's call for caution when addressing 'Judaism' – and 'religion' in general – as well as Jacob Neusner and Daniel Boyarin's contributions to the topic, in this article I reassess the Greek Testament of Levi as well as its 'older brother,' the Aramaic Levi Document. Liberated from the chains of binary thinking, a new, cultural-evolutionary approach based on the theory of Robert Bellah sheds new light on these texts and their possible contexts.*

The other day when I was reading the *Times of Israel* I came across a blog by Rabbi Elyse Goldstein on observing the fast on Tisha B'Av, or to be more precise, on her apology for why she was not fasting. Her reasoning was relevant for this contribution and the general theme of the volume. Tisha B'Av commemorates the destruction of the First and Second Temples. As Goldstein explains, "those destructions also marked the end of the priesthood and the sacrificial system. The end of the supposed 'unity' of a people with one national shrine, one national ritual, one national way of worshiping. I am a rabbi. I won't be fasting." It would of course be superfluous to advocate that this supposed 'unity' did not exist; it is now commonly accepted that at the time there was a wide variety of forms of Judaism.[1] Before I set down my criticism of Goldstein's apology, here is the core of her argument:

> I'm not fasting because the oldest symbol of that so-called 'unity' – the Western Wall – is a battleground for religious pluralism, and I imagine that if the kohanim were still around, they would be on the side of the Haredim, not on the side of those women who, like me, want to be full participating Jews ... And I'm not

1 See for example Satlow 2006, 837-860; Boyarin 2002, 427-461; and more recently Id. 2015; furthermore Mimouni 2015, 113-147 and Mason 2007, 457-512, as well as Vinzent 2014. On more 'classical' views on varieties within Judaism see for example Neusner 1985, 2000; Goodman 2011, 419-434, and Id. 2009, 202-213. An interesting perspective is offered by Rutgers 2016, 167-196, as well as Ilan 2009, 363-395.

> fasting because, ultimately, the destruction of the Temple lent way for the democratization of Judaism, wrestling power and authority out of the hands of an elite and corrupt priesthood and placing it in the hands of scholars, and then rabbis, who represent the people. Eventually in our day, all Jews have the authority to be their own priests, to hold holiness in their own hands, to read their own Psalms as they ascend the stairs of their synagogue, to lead their own prayers, and even to make their own halachic decisions. I celebrate that democratization. ... I don't mourn the loss of a hierarchical, inherited caste of priests – I would, however, mourn the loss of democracy.[2]

Goldstein's plea offers an excellent invitation to address the 'We' versus 'They' theme, as well as themes that are represented in both the *Aramaic Levi Document* (*ALD*) and the Greek *Testament of Levi* (*T.Levi*). I will not enter into the discussion of the nature of women as full participating Jews, but ideas of inclusion and exclusion – by birth, by circumcision – are clearly present in *T.Levi*, where for example the author narrates the disappointment of the father with regard to his sons' revenge on Shechem after the rape of their sister Dinah not because of the nature of their offence, but because the perpetrators had been circumcised before they were murdered;[3] in other words, Levi and his brother had murdered fellow Jews. Then there is the section on the rejection of exogamy,[4] as well as concerns about purity:[5] aspects which might reflect debates on these topics that were current, and which are, interestingly, still topics of debate today. Where Goldstein speaks about democratization of Judaism, in *T.Levi* we could interpret the author's revision of the Levite priesthood as a democratization of the priesthood, yet it remains Levite. Furthermore, while *T.Levi* offers a criticism of the priesthood, the texts also reflect the diversity of Judaism; one has to be aware, and this is contrary to Goldstein's apparent perception, that not all forms of Judaism were Temple-centered. Robert Bellah's ideas of axial breakthroughs that enabled diversification, local differences, and diaspora identities are relevant here.[6] Judaism before the destruction of the First and Second temples was not the 'unity' criticized but at the same time endorsed by Goldstein, and the destruction was not such a watershed that it led to the democ-

2 Goldstein 2016.

3 T.Levi 6, 3-8: "And after this I counselled my father, and Reuben my brother, to bid the sons of Hamor not to be circumcised; And I slew Shechem first, and Simeon slew Hamor. And my father heard these things and was wroth, and *he was grieved in that they had received the circumcision*, and *after that* had been *put to death*." (The italics are mine.)The translation here and in subsequent quotations is from Charles 1913.

4 T.Levi 9, 10-11: "Take, therefore, to thyself a wife without blemish or pollution, while yet thou art young, and not of the race of strange nations." This testifies to the Testament's strongly Jewish character, and one may ask why a Christian redactor would have preserved it.

5 See, for example, T.Levi 8; 9; 14.

6 Robert Bellah (1927-2013) was an American sociologist famous for his work on social theory, religion, culture, and societies, and in particular for his work on the "axial age", see most recently Bellah and Joas 2012.

ratization of Judaism; rather Goldstein's idea of democratization already existed in the myriad local differences and variety of Jewish 'diaspora identities' which may be explained in the framework of axial breakthroughs. It was not the destruction of the Temple that triggered this process. One may also think of the discussions in Paul, or the never-ending question 'who is a Jew?' – both of which testify that before the destruction Jews did make their own halakhic decisions and that rabbinic Judaism did not emerge immediately afterwards, rather that it was a marginal group which developed gradually and then subsequently claimed its own authority and supremacy.[7] In a way, one could argue against Goldstein that rabbinic Judaism eventually put an end to the democratization of Judaism. In addition, Goldstein seems to suggest that only one form of Judaism survived, namely rabbinic Judaism. Her perspective comes to the fore when she urges the reader to remember that "from the ashes of the Temple rose the phoenix of rabbinic Judaism, and that's the Judaism I now celebrate, the Judaism that survived."[8] As such, she is committing the same fallacy as those whom she criticizes. Furthermore, and here one is presented with another we–they fallacy, Goldstein claims that "in a way, the very existence of the rabbis and the Talmud undermined the Temple. To rebuild the Temple would undermine the existence of an interpretive Judaism. The Pharisees won in the end, and interpretation won too over the fixed, hegemonic ritual of the Sadducees."[9] Of course, this is the rhetoric of an op-ed piece in an online newspaper, not an academic argument; still, it reveals the tendency to read the sources in a way that fits one's own denominational interest.[10] It reflects what Michael Satlow has called first-order essentialist speaking about religion.[11] Again, this may be tolerable in a rabbi's

7 Cf. Cohen 1999, esp. 25-68; Satlow 2008; Boyarin 1997, 39, 59, 159-160. For references to discussions that reveal a 'diversification' of Judaism or 'democratic' Judaism in Paul, see for example Rom 15:27, Gal. 4.

8 Goldstein, op.cit.

9 Ibid.

10 Another fine rhetorical example of Goldstein's point of view is the following: "Israel is the living reality of a people .... Fasting on Tisha B'Av almost seems like a slap in the face to that sovereign Jewish nation. I want to imagine that if the Rabbis of the Talmud were living today, they'd say, 'what? How can you keep a fast that longs for a nation you are living in now?'" With all due respect for Goldstein's attempt to defend the legitimacy of the State of Israel, projecting the modern concept of nation-state onto antiquity is problematic to say the least. Goldstein's interpretation of rabbis as well as the effects of 66-70 (the first Roman–Jewish War) are also problematic, since the uprising in the Diaspora (115-117) and particularly the ferocity of the Bar Kokhba Revolt (132-135 CE) offer unmistakable evidence that the very hope Goldstein dismisses already in 68 is very much alive, even in the immediate aftermath of the destruction of the Second Temple.

11 Satlow 2006, 843. First-order essentialist speaking of religion signifies in-group self-understanding, as Satlow explains: "First-order self-definitions are useful as data; they tell us about a group's self-perception. They are, however, far less useful as analytical or explanatory scholarly categories. First-order definitions of 'Judaism' do not seek to describe a religious phenomenon but to create an 'authentic' community by drawing lines between 'orthodox' and 'heterodox' manifestations (cf. Boyarin 2004: 22-26). They are inherently normative. Such definitions might be entirely

apology for why she is not fasting on Tisha B'Av, but it is different when one observes a similar tendency in academic scholarship.

## Modern scholarship and the politics of the modern 'We'

In order to put this contemporary anecdote into context, with emphasis on the context of Levi, I will briefly address the problems and questions raised by modern scholarship on Levi. Scholars have been immensely influenced by categorical and binary thinking, which skews their interpretations of ancient texts and material. This is the dilemma of the we–they or us/them problem to which the current volume is dedicated. One reviewer pointed out that we can only argue that categorical and binary thinking distorts our perspective by ourselves constructing an 'us' that others those who defend the binary perspective. One fine example is the current 'Radical Perspective on Paul,' which seeks to situate Paul the Jew firmly within Judaism, against scholarship either from a Christian denomination that regards Paul as the founder of Christianity, the one who breaks away from Judaism, or from a traditional Jewish perspective that seeks to portray him in a remarkably similar fashion, though with less positive connotations. This illustrates another level of us/them in the context of modern scholarship, but it also shows that a mechanism of 'otherization' is almost inevitable when one enters into a discussion, be it with moderns or with ancients.

A particularly strong and persistent urge to dichotomise is often present when there is a question of what is perceived as 'Jewish'/'Judaism,' versus 'Christian'/'Christianity'. As a matter of fact even our definition of religion problematizes our interpretation of ancient expressions of 'religious' experience, identity, or affiliation.[12] The question then pertains: why were, and why are, so many scholars determined to fit *T.Levi* (and *ALD*) into the preconceived – yet retrospectively developed and projected – categories of either 'Jewish' or 'Christian,' and how do those categories relate to contemporary identity politics?

Since the thirteenth century, the question at the core of research into the *Testaments of the Twelve Patriarchs* (*T12P*), including *T.Levi*, has been: "are we dealing with a Jewish or a Christian document?"[13] Scholarship is divided when it comes to the dating and denomination of *T.Levi*, and there is no agreement as to the determination of its author, audience, and redactor(s). It is therefore necessary briefly to introduce the two main camps before I add my own interpretation. The standard view is that *T.Levi* is a Jewish text with later Christian interpolations. The opposing view is that it is a Christian text that makes use of older Jewish traditions. Instead of subscribing to either of

---

appropriate for the community that wishes to define itself, but they are less appropriate for the academic student of Judaism who seeks to develop descriptive and analytical models."

12 The "different categories" mentioned in the conference argument rightly suggest that awareness is needed, but this does not mean we cannot speak relevantly about these ancient texts and times. Cf. Rüpke and Rebillard 2015.

13 This question was of course formulated in a multiplicity of ways.

these hypotheses, I challenge both on the ground of their basic assumption that a clear distinction between Jewish and Christian identities existed at the time.

## Greek *T.Levi* from *T12P*

*T.Levi* was transmitted as part of *T12P*, and considered to belong to the genre of *Pseudepigrapha*. The manuscript's exact origins are contested, but there are some interesting parallels with Qumran literature.[14] As for *T.Levi* in particular, it unmistakably reveals its inspirational source as the *Aramaic Levi Document*.[15] I shall not go into detail on the reconstruction hypotheses of *ALD*, but it is important to acknowledge that most scholars agree that *ALD* can only, or in Marinus De Jonge's words can *best*, be reconstructed on the model of the Greek *Testament*, although its exact form cannot be determined.[16] The connection between the two literary bodies has most elaborately been demonstrated by Robert Kugler in his monograph *From Patriarch to Priest*, where he illustrates the development from *ALD* through *Jubilees* to *T.Levi*.[17] Rather than repeating what has already been proven, in this contribution I seek to test what happens when both textual bodies are studied from the perspective of a new methodology: a cultural-evolutionary approach.

Research on *T.Levi* has mostly subscribed to one of two approaches. Scholars like Wilhelm Bousset[18] and Marc Philonenko[19] propagate the 'standard' view that *T.Levi* is originally a Jewish text that was picked up by a Christian author, who 'Christianised' it by inserting typical 'Christian' typologies. The weight of this scholarly argument is noticeable in the various text editions and translations, where we find brackets in the text where scholars or editors have agreed Christian interpolations appear.

The opposition to this 'standard' view holds that *T.Levi* is thoroughly Christian. Among this group scholars like Marinus de Jonge[20] and Michael Stone[21] have argued,

---

14 Slingerland 1977, 44ff; consider also Klawans 2006, 145-174; Kugler 2008, 5-23; Kugel 1993, 1-64; as well as Werman 1997, 211-225. In this context it is also worth comparing Swartz 2001, 182-193, as it indicates possible parallels between T.Levi and Hekhalot Rabbati. Compare Alexander 2006, who dedicates a chapter to the relation between Hekhalot mysticism and Qumran.

15 Greenfield, Stone, Eshel 2004.

16 De Jonge 1999, 89.

17 Furthermore, Kugler suggests that T.Levi might have existed independently before its incorporation into T12P; see Kugler 1996, 224.

18 Bousset 1900a, 141-175. See also his argument, partially picked up by Kugler about a century later, that one can detect a Jewish Grundschrift; Bousset 1900b, 187-209.

19 Philonenko 1960.

20 See for example De Jonge 1960, 182-235.

21 Stone 1991, 259-270, at 262: "T12P is basically a Christian composition incorporating earlier Jewish sources and writings. This view is nicely confirmed in the case of the Testament of Levi, for Aramaic fragments and parts of a Greek translation of what seems to have been one of its sources have survived. That source stemmed in our view from the third pre-Christian century at least." I appreciate that T.Levi relies heavily upon or borrows from ALD, but that still does not justify the claim that T.Levi is a Christian composition.

at least for the Greek *T.Levi*, since it was included in and transmitted through *T12P*, that text, author, and audience were Christian rather than Jewish. According to them, a Christian author made use of a variety of older, Jewish material to compose the *Testament*. It was a Christian text by a Christian hand for a Christian audience, although the author was seemingly acquainted with, and had access to, Jewish literary sources.

Unfortunately, both views reflect the problematic binary divide of an already well-established rupture between an identifiably different 'Judaism' versus 'Christianity'. It is time for a new approach. As early as 1960 the philologist and Biblical scholar F. M. Braun challenged both views, which in turn led to extensive criticism from De Jonge.[22] Braun stated that one cannot legitimately speak of *T.Levi* as being either Jewish and interpolated, or Christian and based on a variety of older Jewish sources.[23] Rather, he wrote, one should speak of a Jewish '*Grundschrift*' which was later *redacted* by Christians.[24] Still, even Braun's approach holds on to a presupposed dichotomy between a Jewish and a Christian identity, and as such one could postulate that he also presupposes an already established institutionalization of identities at the time of the supposed redaction of the (earlier) texts. However, looking at the *textus receptus* this idea of Christian redaction can hardly be defended. There is only one explicit mention of a Christ-figure in *T. Benjamin* 10.7-10, and Christ is only referred to once in *T12P*, namely in *T.Levi* 10.1,. *T.Levi* 10.1-5 reads:

> 10.1 Now, therefore, observe whatsoever I command you, children: for whatsoever things I have [2] heard from my fathers I have declared unto you. And behold I am clear from your ungodliness and transgression, which ye shall commit in the end of the ages [against the Saviour of the world, Christ, acting godlessly], deceiving Israel, and stirring up against it great evils from the [3] Lord. And ye shall deal lawlessly together with Israel, so He shall not bear with Jerusalem because of your wickedness; but the veil of the temple shall be rent, so as not to cover your [4] shame. And ye shall be scattered as captives among the Gentiles, and shall be for a reproach [5] and for a curse there. For the house which the Lord shall choose shall be called Jerusalem, as is contained in the book of Enoch the righteous.

The redactors have put between brackets the clause '…against the Saviour of the world, Christ, acting godlessly…' to indicate a suspected gloss. In *T.Benjamin* the phraseology is less explicit:

---

22 See Braun 1960, 516-549 and De Jonge's criticism of Braun: De Jonge 1962, 311-319.

23 Braun 1960, 516-549.

24 In line with Braun, see also Becker 1980; 1970; Hultgård 1977, 1981; Kee 1983, 775-828; Ulrichsen 1991. All argue that with the text is a Jewish Grundschrift that was expanded in a Greek version and finally underwent a Christian redaction; see Collins 1984, 134. See also Kugler 1996, who tries to reconstruct the pre-Christian Greek document based on Aramaic Levi, which he then dates to the Hasmonean period and the reign of John Hyrcanus II, a hypothetical document which he calls 'Original T.Levi'.

> 10.5 … For all these things they gave us for an inheritance, saying: Keep the commandments of God, until the Lord [6] shall reveal His salvation to all Gentiles. And then shall ye see Enoch, Noah, and Shem, and Abraham, and Isaac, and Jacob, rising on the right hand in gladness. [7] Then shall we also rise, each one over our tribe, worshipping the King of heaven, [who appeared upon earth in the form of a man in humility. And as many as believe on Him on the earth [8] shall rejoice with Him]. Then also all men shall rise, some unto glory and some unto shame. And the Lord shall judge Israel first, for their unrighteousness; [for when He appeared as God in the flesh to deliver them they believed Him [9] not]. And then shall He judge all the Gentiles, [as many as believed Him not when He appeared [10] upon earth]. And He shall convict Israel through the chosen ones of the Gentiles, even as He reproved Esau through the Midianites, who deceived their brethren, [so that they fell into fornication, and idolatry; and they were alienated from God], becoming therefore children in the portion of them that fear the Lord.

The wording in *T.Benjamin* does not use 'Christ' explicitly, but seems to refer to a Christ-figure, hinting at the incarnation. These clauses are again put in between brackets to indicate a possible gloss.

I might suggest that one scribe wrote it in the margins, the next copyist put it in the main body of text. The fact the first scribe glossed the text suggests they regarded it as 1) not Christian enough, so it needed glossing, but 2) Jewish enough to be worth endorsing: they recognised it as something to which they subscribed, as "part of the Jewish race". This phrase appears in *T.Levi* chapters 14-15; 14.4 explicitly mentions the identification of Jews as belonging to a distinct Jewish race. De Jonge argues that Christ is implied in these fragments, but that already shows him reading too much into them. Although the text has been glossed, it is important that the typologically 'Jewish' characteristics have not been edited out, meaning that we cannot strictly dichotomize between 'Jews' and 'Christians' yet. Although Braun is stricter in his judgment and sees 'Christian' redaction – I would not label it as such – his argument is to be favored over the other two alternatives. He attempted to analyze *T.Levi* using textual criticism, for which he was rebuked by De Jonge (see also below), who stated that the textual composition of the manuscripts is so complicated that textual criticism is not possible. Braun is still closer to the mark, however, since he accepts both *ALD* and *T.Levi* as Jewish; he only adds that at a later stage in their reception history they were redacted by Christians who started to use these texts. The latter development has been studied by Bryan A. Stewart, who investigated how the Levite priesthood evolved (and developed) beyond the second century, as well as how it was culturally adopted (and adapted) by later emerging Christian groups as they read it in the context of authors like Tertullian, Cyprian, Origen, and Eusebius.[25]

This debate between an alleged 'old' and a 'new' framework seems somehow misleading, as it assumes an institutionalization of identities that did not exist at the time of composition. Instead, we have to look at the text itself as expressing a rather particular,

25 Stewart 2015.

perhaps even individual, interpretation of the loss of the Temple of Jerusalem and the new ways of understanding the task and standing of priests. We can then derive some insights into the complex reality of a society where boundaries between various religious groups were blurred at the very least, and freedom for creative developments came about. This is a phenomenon characteristic of "axial breakthroughs," of axial age societies (a term first coined by Karl Jaspers), and signifies a pivotal period in which societies across Eurasia, although not directly connected, were restructured by new, similar developments in forms of thinking.[26]

As mentioned above, De Jonge criticized Braun's approach, stating that textual criticism is not possible for the *T12P* because of its complicated manuscript history;[27] but De Jonge allows literary criticism, which means considering what the text tells us as it stands, without immediately having to speculate about later redactions. As already suggested, the debate of Jewish *versus* Christian is misleading: one should not approach sources from an institutionalized framework, but think of them in their own terms, as composed by individual agents with a particular agenda, embodied in their complex socio-historical context. This implies a socio-anthropological background of lived experience where views that to us seem opposed, and which modern scholars thus explain as 'interpolations,' might at the time have represented views that the author and audience could easily identify with. That is to say, returning to the we–they or us/them theme: in the ancient context, views that would for us clearly testify to a singular Jewish or exclusively Christian identity might have been perfectly acceptable for someone identifying as belonging to either or none of these denominations in antiquity – obviously also differentiating between readers and redactors (those who used the texts) in the first, second, third, and fourth centuries CE.[28] The bracketing of the *textus receptus* is evidence, as mentioned earlier, of preconceptions that cannot accept the possibility that self-identifying Jews could also refer to a Christ-figure. Conversely, self-identifying Christians would not accept the law; therefore the text must originally be Jewish.[29] These are only two illustrations, but they question the way we portray 'them'.

### Beyond binary thinking and denominational essentialism

After having demonstrated the problems that prevail in previous scholarship, I will now try to apply a combination of Michael Satlow's observations on defining religion (and

26 Jaspers 1949. The period runs from the eighth until the third century BCE. See also Bellah 2005. As Momigliano has it: the axial age is the age of criticism, as quoted in Bellah 2005, 72.

27 De Jonge 1962.

28 Challenges to these segregating categories have repeatedly been phrased by Daniel Boyarin; see for example Boyarin 2002, 2004, 2015; Boyarin and Barton 2016.

29 My reservations regarding such preconceptions and my intention to challenge these dichotomies finds resonance in Boyarin and Barton's conclusion, entitled "What you find when you stop looking for what isn't there"; see Boyarin and Barton 2016.

Judaism in particular) and Robert Bellah's paradigm of 'cultural evolution'.[30] This will allow me to reassess authorial self-identification in *T.Levi* and its 'older brother', *ALD*. The texts thus become witnesses in their own right of the rich diversity of religious groups and the relative freedom of what would later be called 'syncretistic' activities of religious individuals (perhaps not too far from contemporary individual religious freedom), even when they seem to adhere to the same religion.[31]

Satlow points out the tension inherent in understanding a religion as a unified tradition, in light of the diversity in the thought and practice of actual lived religious communities.[32] This adds value to Bellah's cultural-evolutionary approach. To address this tension, Satlow suggests, following Jonathan Z. Smith, that scholars should develop a map of characteristics: a polythetic model that accounts for a wide diversity of actual religious manifestations while at the same time requiring the development of the basic map of characteristics that underlie a single 'religion.'[33] In a variety of Judaisms, each appears as a shifting cluster of characteristics that varies over time.[34] As Satlow iterates: "a community's Judaism is not made by a collection of texts or norms but by historically and socially situated human beings who engage, filter, and activate their traditions according to their local understandings."[35] If one adds Bellah's ideas of cultural evolution, it will set the text, its author, and audience free from thinking in terms of static religious institutions or traditions. It will enable us to see a continuous line of development between *ALD* and *T.Levi*; the shifting contexts witnessed by the author and audience of Greek *T.Levi* called into question authority, power, political power, identity, and hierarchy. Furthermore one does well to remember that, as Satlow again pointed out, "Church fathers constructed 'Judaism' as an antonym to 'Christianity' as a definable entity that contained an identifiable essence and stood in relationship to 'Christianity'.

---

30 Bellah also refers to Bruner, who has remarked that narrative actually constitutes the self: "the self is a telling. Not only do we get to know persons by sharing our stories, we understand our membership in groups to the extent that we understand the story that defines the group." Bellah 2005, 85. For Satlow's paradigm, see Satlow 2005, 2006, 2008.

31 This could hint at linguistic barriers between 'us' and 'them.'

32 Satlow 2006. Compare Bellah's understanding of religion as a set of symbolic forms and acts that relate people to the ultimate conditions of their existence (Bellah 1964, 359), and Geertz (in Satlow 2006), who interprets religion as a system of meaning; other scholars see religions as cultural repertoires that agents use "in complex, varying ways on various occasions, shifting the cultural framing of a problem in mid-discourse" (see Campany 2003, 318, quoted in Satlow 2006, 845). Neusner privileges rabbinic Judaism (like Goldstein), which according to Satlow sits uneasily within his fuller conceptual model (Satlow 2006, 845).

33 Mapping of characteristics, or mapping of concepts, refers to the visualizing of patterns and relationships in a model – for which the software programme CMap can be used. An example by Satlow can be seen at http://mlsatlow.com/2012/04/05/mapping-the-talmud/ (last accessed: 27.09.2017).

34 Satlow 2006, 845; Smith 1982, 18.

35 Satlow 2006, 846.

This is a colonial understanding,"[36] and a construction that continues to exert influence over scholarship today. It is pertinent that up until the medieval period Jewish writers never seemed to use the term 'Judaism' to denote a complete religious system.[37]

Researchers have already analyzed *T12P's* parallels with the Dead Sea Scrolls and similar Jewish and Christian literature.[38] As far as I am aware, however, no attempts have been made to analyze *T.Levi* in the context of emerging Jewish mysticism, where once the earthly Temple was destroyed and the city of Jerusalem lost, the spiritual focus shifted to the heavenly realm. Nor have any attempts been made to approach the text as a response to the atrocities experienced by the Jewish people between 70 and 135 CE. The texts have not been examined using a methodology of religious agency either. Dereck Daschke, adopting a psychoanalytical perspective, has shown how apocalyptic literature more generally can be read as a response to the destruction of the Temple and Jerusalem.[39] Similarly, Joshua Johnson has tried to approach this literary genre from a perspective of trauma studies.[40] In what follows I have tried to read *T.Levi* as a *Jewish* response not only to the destruction of the Temple but also to the defeat of the revolt.[41] Bellah's axial age theory is useful here. There is reason to believe that for centuries people felt prompted, given the loss of the Temple and the loss of Jerusalem, to seek new ways to access God and to (re)establish the relation between Israel and its creator: an existential quest that required a rethinking and reshaping that would lead to a new understanding of Jewish identity. In *T.Levi* this happens in a thorough revision or redefinition of priesthood, implying a 'cultural evolution.'

---

36 Satlow 2006, 840. First-order definitions are created by communities for their own definitional purposes (e.g. Goldstein); see Satlow 2006, 842. Compare Neusner's second-order definition of Judaism as a religious system that can best be described through attention to its ethnos, ethics, and ethos (Satlow 2006, 843; Neusner 1993, 8). Thomas Hunt has drawn our attention to the prominence of colonialism and colonial thinking in much of the scholarship from the nineteenth up to the mid-twentieth century; it influenced not only how research was conducted, but also how sources were interpreted and for what reasons, see Hunt 2018.

37 Satlow 2006, 84;, see also Boyarin 2004, 21-57.

38 For a comprehensive account of the history of research on *T12P*, see Slingerland 1977; more recently a concise account has been published by Kugler 2001. For a more general but incredibly comprehensive overview of research into pseudepigrapha, see DiTommaso 2001.

39 Daschke does not specifically single out the destruction of the Second Temple and the defeat of the Bar Kokhba Revolt, but considers apocalyptic literature as reaction both to the destruction of the First Temple and the Babylonian exile and to the destruction of the Second Temple. See Daschke 2010.

40 Johnson 2012.

41 I do not claim there was no earlier Greek *T.Levi*, but the text as it now stands could well have been amended – based possibly on earlier sources, and possibly not only *ALD* but maybe a Greek Levi text too – to fit the post-135 situation; however this is still not solid evidence that the text is Christian. The author and his audience self-identify as Jewish, explicitly.

### Cultural-evolutionary theory as a liberation of Levi

The problem with applying Bellah's theory to these texts is that their historical contexts are situated in what he defines as the axial age, or the stage of "historic religions."[42] Yet the problem of having to detect an evolution within a single period can be solved by combining Bellah's with Satlow's model. Of course, calling this period 'axial' does not reflect at all how 'they' (the ancients) perceived their own day and age. This terminology only reflects our validation of this time as crucial for our own understanding, and perhaps self-understanding. Back in 1975 Eric Weil touched upon the problem of "we vs they," arguing that the axial is culturally autobiographical. He illustrates his argument by showing that whenever *we* discover something about a relatively unknown religious group, we immediately connect it to a tradition that is familiar to us, even though this group (*they*) might not have accorded it such historical importance in their own times. To quote Weil:

> ... the history we write is always at bottom our own intellectual and political autobiography, an attempt to come to a genetic understanding of our own way of living, acting, and feeling. The meanings of terms such as "break through" and "axial time" become clear only if we use them in this context, if we acknowledge that the importance of events and dates is determined by the place we assign to them in our autobiography, and not by their material weight. Any fact is as good as any other so long as we adhere to a plan by which facts are merely defined as that which existed in the past.[43]

Accurately, Weil states that we refuse to consider ourselves as principal spectators, but insist on our role as actors – the latter implying participation and first-hand knowledge.[44]

---

42 In Bellah's evolutionary theory, evolution is understood as "a process of increasing differentiation and complexity of organization which endows the organism, social system or whatever the unit in question may be, with greater capacity to adapt to its environment so that it is in some sense more autonomous relative to its environment than were its less complex ancestors" (Bellah 1964, 358). In other words, evolution is to be seen as "the simple empirical generalization that more complex forms develop from less complex forms .... What evolves is religion as symbol system" (Bellah 1964, 359). His scheme of religious evolution "is based on several presuppositions: 1) religious symbolization of the general order of existence; 2) conceptions of religious action in society tend to change in ways systematically related to the changes in symbolization; 3) changes are related to a variety of other dimensions of change in other social spheres which define the general process of sociocultural evolution" (Bellah 1964, 360). Bellah distinguishes five stages of evolution: primitive, archaic, historic, early modern, and modern, where historic religions (other than archaic) are all in some sense transcendental (Bellah 1964, 361-366). In historic religions, the religious goal of salvation is for the first time the central preoccupation – hence in Levi the criticism of sinful actions of priesthood. The stages of religious evolution are "based on the proposition that at each stage the freedom of personality and society has increased relative to the environing conditions" (Bellah 1964, 374). "Historic religion is associated with the emergence of differentiated religious collectivities as the chief characteristic of its religious organization" (Bellah 1964, 367).

43 Weil 1975, 22.

44 Weil 1975, 22-23 (italics are mine).

What would be the consequences of applying these insights to the text of *T.Levi*? As already noted, *T.Levi* was influenced by the Aramaic *Levi*. Memory and the act of remembering, the attempt to make sense of events, often takes the form of reaching back in history to narratives composed in light of similar events. The Aramaic *Levi* and related texts mourn the destruction of the First Temple, and hence provide a framework for interpreting the destruction of the Second Temple for the author and audience of *T.Levi* (as it stands in the form transmitted to us). The author of *T.Levi* touches upon themes that reflect identity issues, such as destruction, defeat, and exile. Emphasis is put on the centrality of Torah for the group or textual community and the idea of the ethnic designator of the Jewish race. Furthermore, there are messianic tropes: the text narrates an ideal priesthood or sacerdotalization, while the author claims divinely appointed authority, and comments on group-corrosive iniquities (anti-social behaviour; morality).[45] The author perceives and revises Jewish identity as a reaction to the lived experience of, and existential questions raised by Jews who had directly or indirectly witnessed their society's destruction and the defeat.[46] There is a clear endeavour on behalf of the author to preserve a culture and social organization at a point in time when it was perceived to be threatened.[47]

## Cultural-evolutionary theory applied to the Greek Testament of Levi

What does this mean concretely for a comparison of the texts of *ALD* and *T.Levi*?[48] While the Aramaic text focuses on the ritual of sacrifice and wisdom, partially copied by the author of *T.Levi*, the author of our Greek *T.Levi* adds a section which displays a clear Torah orientation (*T.Levi* 13). This, among other characteristics, could support the argument that *T.Levi* is Jewish, yet in a 'transformed' way: cultural aspects and understanding have changed. One way of describing this development is as 'cultural evolution.' I will highlight and compare those segments that deal with the topics of authority, ritual, priesthood, and sacerdotalization, wisdom and Torah, as well as ideas of ethnicity, to show where we might perceive such a cultural evolution.

### *Authority*

A first remarkable development is the stronger claims to authority expressed in *T.Levi* compared to *ALD*. *ALD* contains Levi's prayer to the Lord (for him and his children)

---

45 For group-corrosive iniquities, see for example *T.Levi* 16, where we also find messianic tropes. The author explains how group corrosion, or anti-social behavior, led to the atrocities suffered; there is displacement, and the destruction of the Temple is indicated more strongly in the addition of the phrase "even to the ground," possibly reflecting the events post-132 CE. The author relates this to the behavior of the guilty parties towards "a man who renews the law in the power of the most high," which could be a reference to Christ.

46 *T.Levi* 13:7.

47 E.g. *T.Levi* 13; 18; 19.

48 *ALD* consists of thirteen fragmentary preserved chapters; *T.Levi* consists of nineteen chapters.

to "grant me all the paths of truth … grant me counsel and wisdom and knowledge and strength in order to do what is pleasing to you" (*ALD* 3:4-7). In *ALD* Levi prays to "purify my heart, Lord, from all impurity, and let me, myself, be raised to you." In *T.Levi*'s vision, Levi *is* taken up to the Lord (2:5-6; 5:1-2). There is thus an evolution: although it is stated that "the Most High has heard [Levi's] prayer" (4:2), in Levi's dream vision – which is also divinely appointed, as "the spirit of understanding of the Lord came upon me, and I saw" (2:3) – an angel also says to him that he is granted the authority to teach and minister, "light of knowledge shalt thou light up in Jacob" (4:2-3) and "sun to all the seed of Israel" (4:3) and "counsel and understanding given [to Levi]," so that he "might instruct [his] sons concerning this" (4:5). This divine appointment to teach allows the author to move on to instruct, as a father to his sons. It is, however, clearly situated within the priesthood: the audience identify as Levites. *ALD* also contains a vision, but there are no authority claims (divine appointment), apart from one phrase which reads "Now, see how we made you greater than all/how I loved you more than all flesh/and how we gave you the anointing (greatness) of eternal peace" (*ALD* 4:11). Explicit claims such as those in *T.Levi* were either never there, or have been lost, since we only have fragmentary manuscripts. But in the texts as they now stand, *ALD* has only one reference to an anointing "of eternal peace," whereas in *T.Levi* Levi is given both priestly authority ("blessings of the priesthood," 5:2-3) and royal authority: "shield and sword" (*T.Levi* 5:1) are royal emblems, the property of princes.[49] In *ALD* the overall sense the reader gets from chapter four is one that subjugates royal power to sacerdotal power. In *T.Levi* the cultural (including the political) context has seemingly changed, and both authorities appear to have been granted to Levi. Furthermore, the Jewishness of this text is clear in the assertion of the Lord that Levi is priest "until I come and sojourn in the midst of Israel" (5:3). One would assume a Christian text would have rendered it 'come again'; this phrase holds that the messiah is yet to come. The text does explicitly identify as 'Jewish'; however, the 'Jewish' label is not opposed to a 'Christian' one, but rather situated among a rich diversity of types of Judaism. The same chapter also contains clear references to destruction (of the Temple), and hints about the multiple attacks the Jewish people suffered at the hands of the Romans.

To summarize, the developments at the level of authority appear to be that in *T.Levi* there is more stress on Levi's authoritative role than in *ALD*, which could suggest a changed socio-political context in which power roles shifted and thus needed to be redefined.

### *Ritual, Priesthood, and Sacerdotalisation*

Ritual purity is essential in *ALD*, and it is given much attention. In chapter two, Levi says "I laundered my garments, and having purified them in pure water, I also washed my whole self in living water, and I made all my paths upright" (*ALD* 2:4-5). Furthermore, he prays "Purify my heart, Lord, from all impurity, and let me, myself, be raised to you" (*ALD* 3.13). But the most important reflection on purity appears in chapter six.

49 See for example Kugler 1996, 225.

Levi must be aware of uncleanliness and of all sin, since his judgement is greater than that of all flesh. He is near to God and near to all his holy ones, and therefore must be pure in his flesh from every impurity of man (*ALD* 6:1-5). In *T.Levi* purity appears in, for example, 14:6 ("wedded women shall ye pollute, and the virgins of Jerusalem shall ye defile: and with harlots and adulteresses shall ye be joined, and the daughters of the Gentiles shall ye take to wife, purifying them with an unlawful purification"), 15:1 ("Therefore the temple, which the Lord shall choose, shall be laid waste through your uncleanness"), 16:1-2 ("And now I have learnt that for seventy weeks ye shall go astray, and profane the priesthood, and pollute the sacrifices"), and 16:5 ("And ye shall have no place that is clean"), but as one can see, purity appears in the context of condemnation. In *ALD*, the issue is Levi's own purity; in *T.Levi* the author warns his audience that they will lose their purity, that they will pollute what they touch, that no place will remain that is pure – an essential concern for the practice of the priestly rites, as is evident from *ALD*. What would be left of the priesthood when all (priests, sacred space, women) has been defiled? This is the situation the audience of *T.Levi* are facing, which the author seeks to resolve.

With regard to the sacrifices, there is a development of religious ritual or symbolism. In *ALD* significant attention is paid to the correct execution of offerings in chapters 7-9, whereas in *T.Levi*, sacrifice is far less of a focal point, with only 9:12 referring briefly to the wood offering and 9:13 to animal sacrifice ("... And offer a sacrifice to the Lord of every clean beast and clean bird"). It could be suggested that the offering has been replaced, or resituated from the now destroyed earthly Temple to the heavenly realm, where, according to the author of *T.Levi*, offerings are being brought to the Lord which have "a sweet smelling savour, [and which are] a reasonable and a bloodless offering" (3:5).

Yet it is principally in the development or transformation in the understanding of the office of the priesthood, and thus of religious action in society, that one can argue for cultural evolution, and it is a cultural evolution that implies a democratization of the priesthood. In *T.Levi*'s second vision he is first officiated as priest, then follows the explanation of the three offices of priesthood, and ultimately the failure of the priesthood and the announcement of a new priest. The account of Levi's vision could be interpreted as a process of sacerdotalization with anointment, purification, etc.:

> And I saw seven men in white raiment saying unto me: Arise, put on the robe of the priesthood, and the crown of righteousness, and the breastplate of understanding, and the garment of truth, and the plate of faith, and the turban of the head, and the ephod of prophecy. ... From henceforth become a priest of the Lord, thou and thy seed for ever. And the first anointed me with holy oil, and gave to me the staff of judgment. The second washed me with pure water, and fed me with bread and wine (even) the most holy things, and clad me with a holy and glorious robe. The third clothed me with a linen vestment like an ephod. The fourth put round me a girdle like unto purple. The fifth gave me a branch of rich olive. The sixth placed a crown on my head. The seventh placed on my head a diadem

of priesthood, and filled my hands with incense, that I might serve as a priest to the Lord God. (8:1-11)

The above fragment from *T.Levi* narrates the ideals of priesthood, which, and this is important, remains Levite, and "thou and thy seed" even implies that it remains hereditary. As we can see, Levi gives a vivid image of the priestly garment and the rites of purification,[50] expanding on a corresponding passage in *ALD*, which only has "and [Levi's father] invested me in the priestly garb and consecrated me and I became a priest of the God of eternity and I offered all of his sacrifices" (*ALD* 5:4). Here, then, the comparison of the two texts shows the transformed continuation of a tradition.

Further socio-cultural change and religious development may be found in the explanation of the three offices of the priesthood, which is absent in *ALD*. The high priesthood continues, yet there is a "new name and new priesthood." Since it is one of the three offices of the Levites it is certainly Jewish, but it appears to be an integration of pagan priesthood into the Levite Jewish tradition. We might speculate about complex cultural adaptation here:

> And the third shall be called by a new name, because a king shall arise in Judah, and shall establish a new priesthood, after the fashion of the Gentiles [to all the Gentiles]. And His presence is beloved, as a prophet of the Most High, of the seed of Abraham our father. (8:14-15)

This new priesthood shall be established by a 'king [who] shall arise in Judah', perhaps referring to the installation or restoration of the Hasmonean Kingdom, or even to the Messiah, who creates a Gentile priesthood for the Gentiles. However, it does not necessarily imply the priests are Gentiles themselves; these new priests may have adopted a Gentile fashion in order to reach out to the Gentiles who would otherwise remain 'outcast' – or even to preserve the distinction, so that they need not be fully incorporated, with their own priests to tend to their needs. However, these Gentile priests are still a form of Levites. The passage recalls Paul ("Gentile to the Gentiles"), but not as Paul understood himself: he never calls himself a priest, though in *Romans* 15 priestly typology is used for him. Markus Vinzent has suggested to me that this chapter is not present in Marcion's version of Paul, and seems to have been added to *Romans* around the same time as our proposed date of composition of *T.Levi*.[51] The style and content of *Rom.* 15 fits within the texts and context of mid- to late second-century debates, such

50 According to Tessa Rajak, this fragment underlines the "clearly Jewish" character of T.Levi, in spite of later Christian overlay; indeed, at times it closely follows the so-called Aramaic Levi Document of which we have fragments from Qumran (4Q213-4; 4Q537; 4Q541) and also from the Cairo Genizah. Furthermore, she points at parallels in Ezekiel's vision of ideal priests and the reconstructed ideal Temple, as well as the Merkavah (Ezek 1-10; 40-48); see Rajak 2014, 41-3.

51 The hypothesis is work in progress, but see already Vinzent 2014, 115, where he suggests that in the two collections of Paul's letters Romans would have been the same length, i.e. 1-14, with no 15.

as we find in the Pastoral letters and Ignatius, and seem to not have been a primary concern before that time. Again these parallels indicate that the text may be understood as a post-135 attempt at redefinition.

After a section on teaching, the author picks up the theme of the priesthood again in chapter 17, on the decline of the (Levite) priesthood, and in chapter 18, on the announcement of the new priest, since the priesthood has failed.[52] It will therefore now be concentrated in one new priest: but one who will "lighten the knowledge," meaning the Law will not be abolished but made (even) brighter. This reads as a messianic vision, which fits in with Jewish literature of that time.[53] With this arrival of the new priest Levi becomes a mediator and revelator (chapter 19); the choice presented to his group is between light and darkness, where light is the Torah (the Law, still valid and not made redundant by the messiah), and darkness is Beliar. There is no choice between Torah and the new priest, which is what one might expect from a Christian text. The group have become witnesses, signalling a democratization of the Levite priesthood, which is no longer based on priestly family genealogy. We could speak of a sacerdotalization of the group, or even potentially the multitude.[54]

In summary, in the timespan between *ALD* and *T.Levi* purity became threatened, meaning it was no longer possible to perform the sacrifices correctly, which in *T.Levi* are resituated to the heavenly realm. Purity and sacrifices are intrinsically linked to the priesthood, which is also redefined in *T.Levi*.

### *Wisdom and Torah*

In *ALD* chapter 13 is dedicated to teaching, in the form of poetry: the wisdom poem. Levi orders his sons to "teach reading and writing and teaching of wisdom to your children and may wisdom be eternal glory for you. For he who learns wisdom will (attain) glory through it, but he who despises wisdom will become an object of disdain and

---

Vinzent refers to Marcion's Pauline letter collection and the Marcionite collection that Tertullian knows.

52 Note that criticism of the priesthood is absent in *ALD*, which offers yet another argument for cultural evolution after societal, socio-political, and/or socio-religious change.

53 As Feldman (1993, 294) states, these ideas of a divinely appointed conversion of the Gentiles and universal enlightenment hint at the purpose of spreading the teachings of the Torah to all non-Jews. A parallel can be found in *T.Joseph* 4:4-5; *T.Levi*'s concept of universality could be seen as part of a wider tradition of early Jewish proselytism. See also Goodman 2004, 91-116. It is hardly tenable, then, to consider this a Christian addition. Yet, its continued incorporation indicates that it could still have been read, or at least retained significance, in the context of the post-Marcion debate on the legacy of the Law and the Hebrew Bible/Prophets. In contrast with Marcion, who defied the Law and called it redundant, this Levi text seems to defend the Law.

54 Regarding democratization of the priesthood in *T.Levi*, in light of Bellah 2005, 88: "Breakthroughs involve not only a critical reassessment of what has been handed down, but also a new understanding of the nature of reality, … Weil's argument is that periods of severe social stress, in other words, serious breakdowns, may be the necessary predecessors of cultural breakthroughs." See also Weil 1975 (and above).

scorn" (*ALD* 13:4-5). In *T.Levi*, the author turns to instruction earlier, in chapter 10, yet chapter 13 strongly resembles *ALD* 13. Both authors advocate wisdom as imperishable, a quality that grants admiration, friendship, and honor. In *T.Levi* however, the audience also receive explicit warnings: "But if ye sow evil things, ye shall reap every trouble and affliction" (13:6); "the wisdom of the wise nought can take away, save the blindness of ungodliness, and the callousness (that comes) of sin. For if one keep oneself from these evil things, then even among his enemies shall wisdom be a glory to him" (13:7-8). To this last sentence, the following is added in *T.Levi*, whilst absent in *ALD*: "And in a strange country a fatherland, And in the midst of foes shall prove a friend. Whosoever teaches noble things and does them, shall be enthroned with kings, as was also Joseph my brother" (13:8-9). This passage hints at a situation of displacement which is not present in *ALD* and as such could refer to a societal change, reminiscent of the enforced prohibition of exogamy in *T.Levi* compared to *ALD* (discussed below).

*T.Levi* reflects the central importance of Torah more explicitly than *ALD*, as is clear in these lines:

> And now my children, I command you: Fear the Lord your God with your whole heart, and walk in simplicity according to all His law. And do ye also teach your children letters, that they may have understanding all their life, reading unceasingly the law of God. For every one that knows the law of the Lord shall be honoured. (13:1-3)

Although the priesthood may have been renewed and revised, the Law clearly is not: it keeps its centrality. There is no choice between Torah and the new priest; to choose light is (still) to choose Torah. Conversely, the author concludes the text in chapter 19 with the choice between the Law of the Lord, the light, and the works of Beliar, darkness.[55] The Torah is metaphorically presented as 'light' and those who learn Torah and receive its knowledge are 'enlightened.' More importantly, even in the darkest of times and under the greatest of threats (destruction, deportation, captivity), the Torah will survive and its wisdom cannot be taken away. Here one can detect a parallel with 2 *Baruch*, a Jewish apocalyptic text from the immediate post-Destruction period, which insists that although the Temple is gone, the Jews still have Torah.[56] This could at first

55 Marinus de Jonge, however, points to a possible parallel, particularly because of the author's switch to the first person plural, with Justin's *Dialogue with Trypho* (116:3). Justin "calls the Christian community 'the true highpriestly race of God' … The Christians responsible for the present *T.Levi* saw themselves as the true servants of the true highpriest announced by Levi in chapter 18" (De Jonge 1991, 262). But there is no indication that by "the Law" the author means anything other than Torah: he still refers to the law as the way of light, the right choice. This again controverts the Christian substitution theology interpretation.

56 Schwartz 2007, 32. *T.Levi*, because of its emphasis on the importance of the study of Torah, could be situated in the same context. Schwartz makes a case for *2 Baruch* and *4 Ezra*, which I think may be applicable to T.Levi as well: "Josephus, or the authors of the apocalypses, [who responded] with a renewed embrace of the Torah… both Josephus and the author of *2 Baruch*

sight be interpreted as a rabbinic argument, which holds that whilst the priests are tied to the Temple, the rabbis' study of Torah could take place anywhere. However, the centrality of Torah does not necessarily or automatically hint at a rabbinic context or authorship. Rather, the author turns to Torah because it defines the priesthood, its task and its place in society, and demands that it be obeyed. As such, Torah's centrality is employed to support priestly authority, rather than to reject it. Another indication of a possibly priestly rather than rabbinic context is *T.Levi* 14, which seems to address a debate on Torah, purity, and oral teachings. Levi addresses his group as "lights of Israel" (purer than all the Gentiles), yet warns that they could be darkened by transgression and "bring a curse upon our race." He seems to condemn oral teachings that go against Torah, which are being taught by rivalling groups that could be rabbinic, who "destroy by teaching commandments contrary to the ordinances of God." The author firmly self-identifies as Jewish, as well as identifying their antagonists as Jewish. In chapter 15 Levi seems to blame these groups for the destruction of the Temple and the exile after the revolt; their uncleanness has led to the destruction and the Jewish people becoming "captives throughout all nations." The latter is again a clear reference to the post-135 situation, as it was in reaction to the Bar Kokhba revolt that the Roman Emperor exiled the Jews from Jerusalem and had the province renamed. The post-70 situation was different; it was mostly military figures (and high-ranking officials) who were taken captive and brought to Rome.[57]

To summarize, in terms of wisdom and Torah there is both similarity and development between *ALD* and *T.Levi*. The author of the latter text continues to insist upon the importance of Torah and the priesthood, but one also detects a societal change, perhaps a displacement, which prompts the author to stress the central importance of Torah even more. The priesthood is renewed and revised, but the Law is not.

### *Ethnicity*

*ALD* opens with the story of Dinah, stating that if the sons of [Hamor] desire Jacob's daughter, they should "circumcise [their] fleshly foreskin and look like us, and (then) you will be sealed like us with the circumcision [of tru]th and we will be br[others] for y[ou]." This passage appears in a redacted form in *T.Levi*, but not until chapter six, where the emphasis on circumcision as designator of peoplehood and sign of belonging is strengthened. Whereas *ALD* only states circumcision is required for men to become brothers, which is necessary to marry into a Jewish family, in *T.Levi*, Levi and Simeon go on to commit the murder of Shechem and Hamor. This act is mourned by their father, who "was grieved in that they had received the circumcision, and after that had been put to death" (6:6-7). Circumcision thus marks the border not only between group inclusion and exclusion but also between life and death. The author makes it clear,

---

explicitly polemicized against Jews who had rejected the Torah, implying that this was a common response among literate Jewish survivors of the revolt."

57 See for example Peter Schäfer 2003, particularly the contributions of Benjamin Isaac (37-54), Werner Eck (153-170), and Yaron Eliav (241-277).

through the figure of the father, that homicide of in-group members is illegitimate. This invites the reader to consider – with caution – that if the sons of Hamor had not been circumcised, in other words, had not been Jewish, if their killing would have been justified. Circumcision is not abolished, as one would expect in a Christian text, where circumcision of the heart would supersede circumcision of the flesh; on the contrary, it is made even more significant.

A little further on, in *T.Levi* 9, the ethnic designator is maintained, even emphasized, where it is absent in *ALD*, and exogamy is prohibited when Levi speaks about taking a "wife without blemish or pollution," one who is "not of the race of strange nations." *ALD* contains a similar idea, but here it is situated in the priestly teaching of purity in chapter 6, where Levi is ordered to "marry a woman from my family and do not defile your seed with harlots, since you are holy seed, and sanctify your seed like the holy place since you are called a holy priest for all the seed of Abraham" (*ALD* 6:4). In a parallel passage in *ALD* 11:1 where Levi remembers taking a wife, there is no explicit statement that the wife has to be of the same race. This comparison shows that the ethnic designator is granted greater importance in *T.Levi* than in *ALD*. The author picks up the theme again when he states that although the Levites "be the lights of Israel, (purer) than all the Gentiles," he warns them that they will "bring a curse upon [their] race" (14:3-4) and they will even "take the daughters of Gentiles to wife" (14:6): another statement against exogamy.

To summarise, the absence of the social statement in *ALD* and the more explicit wording and repetition of the prohibition of exogamy in *T.Levi* might allude to a changed sociocultural context in which there existed a greater risk of marriage outside the group. A context of displacement in which Jews were assimilating with their new, "Gentile" environment might be a plausible explanation of this concern.

## Conclusion

It has hopefully become apparent that *T.Levi* has evolved from, developed, changed, and expanded on one of its obvious core sources, the *Aramaic Levi Document*. I regard *T.Levi* as Jewish; it does not self-identify as Christian, but it does show a cultural evolution from sacrifice to (messianic) heavenly realms and democratic priesthood (which however remains Levite). What I have called the 'democratization of the priesthood' in *T.Levi* in that respect accords with Goldstein's narrative.[58]

The Aramaic Levi fragments, their preservation, and the transmission history of *T.Levi* could well be reflected upon in a reception studies manner, by pointing out the circularity of arguments and claims for texts being either 'Jewish' or 'Christian,' or a bit

58 Goldstein's argument being that the democratization of Judaism took place after the destruction of the Temple (see p. 2 above); in T.Levi, as long as the Law is observed, everyone can be a priest or access the heavenly Temple. A similar development may be found in Hekhalot Rabbati, where the exercises, if followed to the letter, allow one to descend to the divine chariot (which could now be understood to be the holy of holies); see Van 't Westeinde 2017.

of both. The author's concern in *T.Levi* is certainly Jewish identity, and the ways this identity is seen and revised in the text could reflect actual concerns felt within Jewish groups that had until recently considered the Jerusalem Temple (and possibly the city) as central to their collective identity. The attempts to annihilate this identity (its culture, its religion), although instigated by outsiders who were Gentiles (non-Jews), are explained in the framework of group-corrosive, immoral behavior of group members themselves. The solution, apart from instruction on how to behave, is the author's return to the centrality of Torah and the ways Temple and the priesthood are narrated or prescribed in the written Law. The myriad forms in which Judaism existed do not allow us to interpret this text as a Christian reaction against Jews; rather, it is a reaction of one Jewish group against another Jewish group. Furthermore, the author still regards Torah as the light; the "light of the Law" provides the "light of knowledge" against the darkness of mankind. The author and audience of *T.Levi* see themselves as belonging to the Jewish race, and their religion is an embodiment of the Torah, a spiritualizing of the Temple, with an emphasis on the Law as Light and Wisdom that will survive all evil, even the disastrous effects of the destruction, defeat, and aftermath of the revolt. The group is thus offered opportunities for survival, and elements of the human capacity to adapt are touched upon, although they are strongly situated or depend on divine agency. Levi is positioned as the mediator between the divine realm and the group, on the grounds of his two visions and the authority he received directly from God and the angels. If the group adheres to his instructions, they will survive and be saved.

It has become clear that these texts breathe ritual: *ALD* offers a detailed description of the ritual practice of sacrifice, *T.Levi* criticizes and transforms ritual, and in her "Why I am not fasting on Tisha B'Av"-text, Goldstein[59] reveals an anti-ritual attitude towards the Temple alongside a pro-ritual attitude concerning the rights of individual Jews. Through the ages the importance of ritual has prevailed, and it resonates in mimetic and narrative culture. If we rely on a 'we' versus 'they' paradigm, we fail to see how much of our life, as Bellah argued, is lived in embodied rituals and practices.[60] In other words: we and they are not all that different, after all.

Finally, to consider the 'we–they' theme from another angle: Levi's claim to authority and criticism reveal a mechanism of 'otherization'. The process of othering is manifested through ritual and through text, in the drawing of boundaries; yet pleas against exogamy are combined with aspects of universalism or democratization triggered by evolved or changed cultural realities. Otherization mechanisms and the impact of historical events shaped not only the ancients' thinking but also our own, and underlie not only we–they but also denominational thinking and advocacy. Furthermore, we need to be aware of the fluidity of traditions, religions, and cultural contexts. If we hold too fast to preconceived paradigms and prejudices we will end up, and this is most certainly the case for the *Levi* texts, in a vicious circle from which we can never escape.

---

59 Goldstein 2016, http://blogs.timesofisrael.com/why-im-not-fasting-on-tisha-bav/ (last accessed: 09.11.2016).

60 Bellah 2005, 85.

# RELIGION AND POLITICS IN THE JEWISH-CHRISTIAN WAR IN SIXTH-CENTURY HIMYAR

PIETER W. VAN DER HORST

**ABSTRACT** *In the years 523-525 CE, a unique war was waged between the Jewish kingdom of Himyar (ancient Yemen) and the Christian kingdom of Ethiopia. The Ethiopians attacked Himyar after the Jewish king began persecuting the Christians in his country. The main sources for the study of this war were all written by Christians and they consistently emphasize the religious motivation of the Jewish king. In this article it is argued that, although religious motives should not be denied, other factors of a more power-political nature probably played a much larger role.*

### The upbeat to the war

In the twenties of the sixth century CE, a short and unique war was waged in the south-western part of the Arabian peninsula. It is unique because, while we know of many hundreds of cases of persecution of Jews by Christians from the last two millennia, we never, or hardly ever, hear of large-scale persecution of Christians by Jews. Yet there is a well-documented – although not well-known – instance in the persecution of the Christians of the city of Najrân by the Jewish king of Himyar in the sixth century.

Himyar is the area of the Arabian peninsula that roughly coincides with present-day Yemen. The Himyarites were one of the largest tribes on the peninsula,[1] and they founded a kingdom in the south-western part in the second–to–first century BCE. In late antiquity the kingdom of Himyar gradually became judaized, at least as far as the elite and the royal family were concerned. We know that by the middle of the fourth century CE there was a sizeable Jewish community in Himyar.[2] Nothing is known with certainty about its origins, but we do know that by the end of the fourth century all traces of polytheism had disappeared from the South-Arabian epigraphic evidence there.[3] When God is referred to in these inscriptions, it is usually with formulae such as

1 According to Pliny the Elder, they were the largest Arab tribe (Nat. hist. 32.161).

2 See the remarks of the fifth-century church-historian Philostorgius in his Hist. Eccl. 3.4-5.

3 Müller 1991, 309: "Immerhin haben in Südarabien die Einflüsse von Judentum und Christentum bewirkt, dass seit der 2. H. des 4. Jh. nach dem Zeugnis der einheimischen epigraphischen Denkmäler der Kult der altsüdarabischen astralen Gottheiten in ihren Tempeln aufhörte und sich, zumindest bei den Herrschern und den Personen gehobenen Standes, welche uns Inschriften hinterlassen haben, die Form eines monotheistischen Bekenntnisses durchsetzte, das weder eindeutig jüdische noch eindeutig christliche Züge trug und somit sowohl von Angehörigen der jüdischen bzw. christlichen Religion als auch voon Anhängern eines lokal geprägten arabischen Monotheismus, dem in manchen Stammesgebieten bereits ein Henotheismus vorausgegangen war, angenommen werden konnte."

'the Lord of heaven and earth' and other similarly Jewish-sounding epithets. In some of these inscriptions we read that the author (or owner) belongs to "the people of Israel" or that God is even designated as "the Lord of the Jews."[4] However, on these stones we never find Jewish symbols such as the seven-armed candelabrum (*menorah*) or the Torah chest (*aron*), symbols that are seen very frequently on Jewish inscriptions from the rest of the ancient world in late antiquity.[5] But the terminology used here is certainly evidence of a judaizing tendency on the Arabian peninsula. Other evidence also points to a considerable growth of Jewish communities both in and outside Himyar, though there is no evidence of any proselytizing, let alone forced conversions.[6]

That situation changes dramatically, however, in the early sixth century. From 522 to 525 CE (perhaps one or two years earlier and later), a strong-willed man was king of Himyar, a man whom the sources variously name Masruq, Dhu Nuwas, and Yusuf As'ar Yath'ar, but he himself preferred the biblical name Yusuf – so I will call him Joseph.[7] Some late Arabic sources assert that he had a Jewish mother who originated from Nisibis, but that remains doubtful; other sources maintain that he had converted to Judaism and demanded that his subjects take the same step.[8] We can only guess at the reasons for this sudden change to the policy of compulsory conversion. Part of his motivation was undoubtedly of a political rather than religious nature. It is highly probable that Joseph wanted to maintain his independence from the two superpowers of his time, the Byzantine and Persian (Sassanid) empires, which continuously threatened his kingdom. And he especially wanted to shake his fist at Ethiopia, the Christian kingdom of Axum, which in the preceding centuries had repeatedly made inroads into his country and tried to colonize it. In Joseph's days, the Ethiopians maintained military settlements in Himyar, officially in order to protect the Christians in the country but in fact for colonialist and expansionist purposes.[9] The fact that many an Ethiopian king, the *negus*, also called himself 'Lord of Himyar' certainly infuriated Joseph. The irredentist expansionism that had been at the core of Ethiopia's foreign policy since the middle of the third century,[10] was undoubtedly the main trigger for Joseph's own aggressive policy of decolonization. Anti-Christian sentiments of a *political* nature therefore played a significant role in his decision to create a Jewish kingdom.

The Christians in Joseph's kingdom – and there were many of them – were shocked.[11] Those in the oasis city of Najrân, where they were the majority, flatly refused to obey the

---

4 Robin 2003, 97-172.

5 See Hachlili 2001.

6 Newby 1988, 24-48.

7 Yusuf was a well-known name among Jews in the more northern part of Arabia, too.

8 Hirschberg 1971, 897-900; the excellent study by Robin 2008 gives all the details.

9 Jones, Monroe 2001, ch. 3; Kobishchanov 1979, 90-108; Drewes 1987; Ryckmans 1956.

10 On this irredentism see Bowersock 2013.

11 On Christianity in Arabia in general see Trimingha 1979. On Himyarite Christianity, Attema 1949; Müller 1991; Robin 2010.

king's command.[12] They felt secure because there was an Ethiopian army unit detached there for their protection. The king succeeded, however, by means of a ruse to have them open the gates of their city for him; the result, after Joseph had tried in vain to persuade the Christians to become Jewish, was a massacre of thousands of Christians in the city and its surroundings.[13]

### The sources

For this part of the story we have four major sources.[14] In chronological order these are: the two Syriac *Letters of Simeon of Beth Arsham*; the anonymous *Book of the Himyarites* in Syriac (and a later Arabic version); and the Greek *Martyrdom of Arethas and his Companions in Najrân* (with later versions in Latin, Ethiopic, Armenian, and Arabic).[15] All four sources were written by Christians (there are no Jewish sources). The background of the *Letters of Simeon of Beth Arsham* is as follows. Late in the year 523, the Byzantine Emperor Justin (518-527) sent his special ambassador for Arab affairs, the high diplomat Abraham, to the Arabian Lakhmid king, or sheikh, al-Mundhir (in Greek sources Alamoundaros), in order to negotiate a peace treaty. Al-Mundhir had successfully fought against the Byzantines in order to maintain his political independence, and he had even taken captive two of the most important generals of the Christian army. In February 524, a peace conference was held in Ramla (in the North-East of the Arabian peninsula), in Al-Mundhir's territory, where an agreement was signed and the two generals were released.[16] But then something completely unexpected took place. A messenger turned up unannounced with a letter from the Himyarite King Joseph to Al-Mundhir. In it, the Jewish king told about the successful persecution of the Christians in his country; he even proudly detailed his atrocities, and he urged not only Al-Mundhir but via him also the Persian king, who was the second addressee of the letter, to do the same and destroy the Christian communities in their territories.

For reasons unknown to us, one of those present was the energetic Christian scholar Simeon of Beth Arsham, a Monophysite priest from Mesopotamia. This man imme-

---

12 On earlier confrontations between Jews and Christians in Najrân in the second half of the fifth century see Müller 1991, 311-312, and Robin 2010.

13 According to the early sources some 4,250 Christians were killed. Later sources mention (much exaggerated) higher numbers.

14 Apart from the sources to be mentioned now we also have a number of shorter remarks on the events in some Christian and (later) Muslim authors: the Greek Christian authors Procopius, Cosmas Indicopleustes, and John Malalas; the Syriac Christian author John of Ephesus; and the Arabic Islamic authors Ibn Ishaq, Ibn Hisham, Ibn al-Kalbi, and al-Tabari. For our purposes they are less relevant, but detailed references can be found in the publications by Beaucamp et al., Robin, and Ryckmans. The four major sources discussed in the main text are dealt with at greater length in Van der Horst 2015.

15 The name Arethas (Arabic Harith) in the title refers to the leading aristocrat of the city's Christian community (not the bishop), who is one of the first to die for his faith.

16 For a detailed reconstruction see Shahid 1964.

diately took notes of what he heard and swiftly sent a detailed letter about the events in Himyar to the patriarch of Alexandria, alomg with a request to come to the rescue of the Himyarite Christians. The Byzantine Emperor Justin also received a copy of the letter. This marked the beginning of the Byzantine intervention in Himyarite affairs. We have this important letter in two versions,[17] though it is still unclear why a second version of this letter was made, for the first version is for the greater part incorporated in it. The second version adds some details but it definitely gives the impression of having been composed by a not much later hand. It was due to this letter that the Ethiopian king, spurred on by the Alexandrian patriarch and the Byzantine Emperor, soon launched a major attack on Himyar, which meant the end of both King Joseph and his Jewish kingdom.

It is important to notice that this letter, our oldest document concerning this persecution, was written very soon after the events, within a couple of months. For that reason it is all the more regrettable that this text has not been preserved in intact form – far from it. Many leaves are missing from the only extant manuscript. In addition, for understandable reasons the author focuses mainly on the cruel acts of King Joseph but hardly at all on what went on before, and of course there is no information on what happened after the persecution because those events took place after he had written his letter. While the second version of the letter has some more details and has been handed down in a somewhat less incomplete form than the first, the same problems apply. For information about matters not mentioned in Simeon's letter(s) we will have to turn to the next (in chronological sequence) major source.

The anonymous *Book of the Himyarites*[18] by and large contains the same information as the *Letter(s),* but it also provides us with some additional data. The most important are undoubtedly the passages in which the counter-attack by the Ethiopian king, Ella 'Asbeha (in Greek Elesbaäs) against Joseph is described: the preparations for the war, the combat between the two armies, the death of the Himyarite king, and the installation of a Christian king by the Ethiopians. This document was also most probably written shortly after the events in the years 523-525, although it already has some more hagiographical traits than the *Letters*. Some scholars have argued that it was again written by Simeon of Beth Arsham, but that has now become untenable. Others argue that the *Book of the Himyarites* was written completely independently from the *Letters*, but that is not probable either. That debate, however, is irrelevant for our purposes. Most unfortunately, this document – again – has been handed down to us in a very incomplete form. We have only one manuscript, and it is very lacunose; large stretches of text are lacking (although it does contain a sort of table of contents), so that again we are robbed of important information. For a more complete picture we have to turn to our fourth source.

17 The first version was published by Guidi 1881, reprinted in Guidi 1945, 1-60. The second version was published 90 years later by Shahid 1971.

18 Moberg 1924 is still the only edition.

The Greek *Martyrium of Arethas and his Companions in Najran*[19] is of a somewhat later date than the Syriac documents just discussed, but according to most researchers it was written within a few decades after the events of 523-525, probably around 550 CE or even earlier. This anonymous text, written by a Monophysite Christian, has been known for a long time (its first edition appeared almost two centuries ago), but the first critical edition of the text, based upon the full manuscript dossier, is recent (see the previous note). There are almost 40 manuscripts, most of them complete. This is the fullest document we have about the dramatic events in Himyar. In spite of its title, the document offers much more than just the martyr stories (which the document has in common with the other sources); it also presents an elaborate and well-informed account of the heavy struggle between the Ethiopian and Himyarite armies and its outcome and aftermath. It will be worthwhile to give a short survey of its contents.

The book was composed as a diptych with a hinge, as well as a prologue and epilogue. Chapters 1-2 form the historical and geographical prologue; chapters 3-23 contain the story of the persecution and thus are the *martyrium* in the proper sense (this first part of the diptych is clearly based upon the first *Letter of Simeon of Beth Arsham*); chapter 24, the hinge, is a song of praise for the city of Najrân; chapters 25-37, the second part of the diptych, describe the events of the war; and chapters 38-39 form the epilogue. It is only in the second part of this diptych that we learn that the Byzantine Emperor enabled the Ethiopian king to attack King Joseph by lending him a large fleet of warships that could transport the Ethiopian army to Himyar. Only here do we learn that after the defeat of the Himyarite army, the Ethiopian king imposed a Christian king on the country and launched a missionary campaign in which the people were forced to adopt Christianity (only to be forced again, a century later, to convert to Islam or else to be deported to either Mesopotamia or Ethiopia; this islamization took place, however, in a period later than that covered by our four literary sources).[20]

These four sources were all written very soon or rather shortly after the events took place and are based upon first-hand knowledge of the affairs. Nevertheless, all of them have their hidden (or not so hidden) Christian agendas and for that reason one cannot simply take the story they present for historical truth. So, for instance, in the Christian martyr stories the suffering of the completely innocent martyrs of Najrân is certainly exaggerated as much as the purely villainous nature of the Jewish king. The picture is too black-and-white. We are nowhere told, for instance, that the Jewish king had good reasons to believe that the Christians of Najrân would support the Ethiopians, his archenemies, in case of an attack on his kingdom. The fact tat they were a 'Trojan horse' in his perception (especially because there were already Ethiopian troops in the city) certainly contributed to his decision to persecute them.

It is also striking that the Christological controversies of the fifth and sixth centuries play a large role in the dialogues between the Himyarite king and his opponents, much larger than one would reasonably expect. They suggest that the king was only interested

19 Detoraki and Beaucamp 2007 is the best edition.

20 A short summary of the events after 525 can be found in Lahey 2007, 609-616.

in religious convictions, not in political issues, although these undoubtedly went hand in hand. But in broad outlines the stories in the four literary sources agree to such an extent that they enable us to reconstruct the main historical events with some probability.

It is still a matter of debate why these events are never mentioned in any Jewish source, ancient or medieval. Some scholars are inclined to attribute this silence to the fact that since the rise of rabbinic Judaism Jewish historiography has come to a standstill. At the end of the first century CE, Josephus was the last Jew to write historical works; after him, no less than 15 centuries passed before Jewish historiography made a hesitant new beginning. A fully satisfactory explanation for this curious phenomenon has still to be found, but the phenomenon in itself could explain the silence on the Jewish kingdom of Himyar in Jewish sources. Another possible explanation is that, since this kingdom was so short-lived and actually turned out to be a failure, very few Jews felt like being reminded of it. It is also possible that Himyarite Judaism, which probably was not very rabbinic in nature, was not regarded as full-blown Judaism by the rabbis and as such was undeserving of a place in the annals of Jewish history. Still another explanation is that the story of Joseph's Jewish kingdom did not fit in with the Jewish self-image, either of that period or later. Stories of Christian persecution of Jews are very numerous, but stories of Jewish persecution of Christians are extremely rare. Jews were persecuted ones, first by Christians and then by Muslims, and their self-image was as victims, not perpetrators. The discrepancy between this self-image as victims of persecution on the one hand and the stories about Jews as persecutors on the other was too difficult to deal with. That might have been one reason to forget this Himyarite episode and not to write about it. Of course, this is yet another speculative theory as well and cannot be proved, but it opens an intriguing perspective in terms of the "we-they" paradigm. It is telling indeed that the first modern Jewish scholar to delve into this subject, Joseph Halévy, most emphatically denied that Joseph could ever have been a Jew![21] It must be added, however, that there are almost no contemporaneous Jewish sources for this time and place in history. For instance, no Jewish sources even mention any of the Jewish tribes that lived in and around Medina and Mecca before and during Muhammad's lifetime, and they do not mention Muhammad's massacre of the Jews in Medina either.

### The main issue between the Jews and the Christians

There is one particular element that catches the eye in our sources. The very first time King Joseph addresses the Christians of Najrân (according to the *Martyrium*), he says that he will save their lives only if they abjure the Trinity, which he regards as a tritheistic (read: polytheistic) form of belief (*Martyrium* 3). Apparently, in Joseph's eyes the doctrine of the Trinity is a denial of the Shema's *Adonai echad* (the Lord is One), which is the core of the Jewish faith. The Najrânites refuse to obey him, arguing in accordance with their Monophysite faith that the Trinity is one Godhead in three manifestations,

---

21 Halévy 1889. For quite a different view see Baron 1957, 63-72 (text), 257-261 (notes); and Robin 2004.

not a plurality of gods. Later, when he has succeeded in entering the city and is interrogating Arethas, the aristocratic leader of the Christians (after whom the *Martyrium* is named), Joseph speaks as follows:

> The Romans understood that he whom our forefathers, the priests and legal experts in Jerusalem, have crucified as a human being because he had blasphemed God (...) was not a God but a human being. (...) Do you think you are better than the Romans who are called Nestorians and who teach us, 'We do not regard him as God but as a prophet of God'? (...) I don't ask you to abjure the Lord of heaven and earth (...), I only want you to say that the crucified one was just a human being, not a God (*Martyrium* 6).

This passage suggests that the early Jewish objection against the deification of Jesus, which is already voiced in the New Testament (John 5.18), was still a major issue in the conflict in Himyar. The fact that Joseph here mentions Nestorians in a positive sense seems stranger than it is. The Nestorians believed that Jesus Christ in fact consisted of two persons, the human Jesus and the divine Logos.[22] This is what Joseph implies when he says that the Nestorians regard Jesus as no more than a prophet of God. Though a somewhat sloppy formulation, it is credible that for him the non-deification of Jesus by the Nestorians, although they were also Christians, sufficed to enable him to try to entice the Christian Najrânites to deny Jesus' divinity themselves. It is noteworthy that after the persecution, the first time we hear again about Christians in Najrân (in later sources), they are Nestorians. King Joseph may indeed have spared Nestorian Christians because they did not deify Jesus in the way other Christians did. However, we cannot be certain that the speech quoted above is a reliable rendering of his words, or even his intentions. It may well be that our Monophysite author, by putting these words into the mouth of the Jewish Joseph, was trying to discredit the Nestorian Christians whom he apparently hated (the Nestorians are presented as the enemy in other passages). It should be kept in mind that orthodox Christians often accused Nestorians of 'Judaism'! The fact that the Christological debates of the fifth and sixth centuries play such a large role in the dialogues between Joseph and the Najrânite Christians leads us to doubt their historical veracity anyway. But that is not to deny that the doctrine of the divine nature of Jesus was in reality a major issue between Jews and Christians in Himyar. After all, it is a perennial issue between the two religions.

Further on, Joseph calls the stubborn Christians fools if they are willing "to die for a man who was a magician and an impostor" (*Martyrium* 8). Here we find a motif (Jesus as *goês kai planos*) that is familiar from Jewish (but also pagan Greek) polemics against Christianity.[23] Later (in §10), Joseph tries to persuade a very prominent and beautiful Christian woman from the city to live with him in his palace, but she reacts by saying that she does not want to have anything to do with someone who calls her God a ma-

22 See Grillmeier 1979, 642-660.

23 See, e.g., Schäfer 2009. For the pagan accusations see, e.g., Cook 2000.

gician and impostor. According to the Jewish king, Jesus was an impostor because, as he repeatedly says, he made himself equal to God (cf., again, John 5.18). Again an early Jewish objection against Christology is put into the mouth of King Joseph, which may indeed have been one of the real problems he had with Christianity.[24]

However much his persecution of the Christians in his country may have been triggered by political motives, one should not deny this king a sincere religious conviction.[25] The fact that the Christian author of this martyrium is completely silent on Joseph's political motivation and has him participate, in a sense, in the christological debates of the sixth century, is a clear sign of that author's Christian bias. The anti-Christian attitude of Joseph was probably primarily a consequence of the continuous aggression and attempts at colonization of Himyar on the part of the Ethiopian kings. Joseph's religious conviction helped justify his own counter-aggression, a phenomenon we witness so often in history, and in our own times.

24 See Gajda 2009. A brief summary of this book can be found in Gajda 2010.

25 Müller 1991, 313: "Das Motiv für die Verfolgung ist wohl nicht nur in religiösem Fanatismus zu suchen, der zweifellos auf Seiten des Königs vorhanden war, sondern auch in einer vom himyaritischen Adel unterstützten fremdenfeindlichen Reaktion gegen eine mögliche Ausdehnung des byzantinischen Einflusses im südlichen Teil des Roten Meeres."

# THE RAPE OF LUCRETIA

## Sanctity of Body and Soul in Augustine

MAKIKO SATO

**ABSTRACT** *In the first book of his City of God (De civitate dei), Augustine discusses the suicide of Lucretia, who killed herself after she was raped. According to his text, the reason for her suicide was her shame. She was afraid of being in the public eye, because people might think she enjoyed her assault. In modern times, too, victims of rape frequently report feeling ashamed. Augustine also mentions Christian women, who were raped and then ridiculed by other people. Augustine says that such people have given no thought to sanctity. Sanctity is sometimes regarded as the same as lack of injury, or purity. Those who ridiculed Christian women who were raped seem to perceive only the women's desecrated state. Augustine, in contrast, argues that the victims still have sanctity, not only in their minds, but also in their bodies. If the sanctity of the victims remains intact, they have no reason to feel ashamed, and it is nonsensical to see them as being in a desecrated state. In this paper, I examine the concept of sanctity in Augustine. Augustine shifts a traditional idea of female purity (pudicitia) to another idea of purity (sanctitas) that is applicable regardless of sex. I will demonstrate that this argument is based on his understanding of the relationship of body and soul. The people whom Augustine tries to refute in the City of God are "worshipers of the many false gods, whom we usually call pagans" (Retractationes 2.43.1). The contrast of "we, Christians" and "they, pagans" is clearly defined. However, Augustine's discussion about women who were raped is applicable to both, because it is the recognition of his own weakness that allows Augustine to see the weakness that every human possesses in their own body and soul.*

## *Pudor* and *pudicitia*

The tale of the rape and subsequent suicide of the Roman matron Lucretia has been "recounted numerous times in a variety of genres across the past 2000 years."[1] As Eleanor Glendinning says, "each author reshaped the story in order to reflect on the pressing political, historical, social and ethical issues of their day."[2] Augustine was among those people. He discussed this famous Roman matron in the first book of his *De civitate Dei*, which concerns the Christian women who were raped in his own time. Just three years before Augustine began this book in 413, the forces of the king of the Visigoths, Alaric, entered Rome (on 24-26 August 410).[3] He writes about the destruction, manslaughter,

1 Glendinning 2013, 70.

2 Ibid., 70.

3 Walsh 2005, 1.

looting, burning, and suffering in the recent sack of Rome.[4] It is natural to think that Augustine knew or believed that people were also raped during this confusion, since "rape was taken for granted in wartime."[5] Of course the victims must have included not only Christians but also pagan Romans. However, at that time, pagan Romans attributed the responsibility for the recent calamity of the world to the Christian religion. They "shamefully and foolishly mocked"[6] Christianity and scoffed at Christians who suffered hardship in the disaster.[7] Augustine's comments on the Roman and Christian women who were raped are made in response to criticism by the pagans, who mocked and accused the Christian victims of rape.[8]

For the Romans, Lucretia was an object of "praises for her chastity (*pudicitia*)."[9] Her suicide after the rape was generally received as the inevitable action of a chaste woman. Not only pagans but also church fathers condoned, or rather praised suicide as a means of retaining chastity.[10] Augustine does not praise victims' suicide. He argues that no one should commit the sin of killing themselves, since killing is forbidden by the Law.[11] In addition, he discusses Lucretia's motivation for suicide, and concludes that it was "not her love for chastity but her weakness of shame (*non est pudicitiae caritas sed pudoris infirmitas*)."[12]

> For she was ashamed that another's foul deed had been perpetrated against her, though not with her consent. And being a Roman woman too eager for praise, she feared that if she continued to live, men would think that she had willingly endured what she actually endured under duress while she was alive.[13]

It may be seen as inhuman to blame a woman who is a victim of rape, though Lucretia was a legendary character and not a real person. One scholar describes Augustine's re-

---

4 August., De civ. D. 1.7.

5 Pellauer 1995, 209.

6 De civ. D. 1.15.

7 See also Shaw 2011, 215-18.

8 De civ D. 1.16: "Our opponents believe that they lay a serious accusation against Christians when they amplify the account of their captivity by additional mention of rape committed not only against other men's wives and against virgins ripe for marriage, but also against a number of consecrated virgins." (Walsh 2005, 57.)

9 De civ D. 1.19.

10 Cf. Ambrosius, De Officiis. 18.68; Je., Adv. Iovinian. 1.49. See also Webb 2013, n. 3.

11 On the sixth commandment, Augustine writes that "it refers to mankind, and includes both others and ourselves" (De civ. D. 1.20). On similarities between Augustine's opinion of suicide and Macrobius', as well as the origins of their discussion in Platonism, see Van der Horst 1971.

12 De civ. D. 1.19.

13 De civ. D. 1.19. (Walsh 2005, 65.) "Puduit enim eam turpitudinis alienae in se commissae, etiamsi non secum, et Romana mulier, laudis avida nimium, verita est ne putaretur, quod violenter est passa cum viveret, libenter passa si viveret."

sponse as a "sneering prosecution."[14] It may actually seem that Augustine condemned Lucretia, a pagan woman, from the viewpoint of a Christian who opposes pagans, while clarifying the conflict between "we, Christians" and "they, pagans." However, Augustine also says that sexual violence "none the less engenders a sense of shame (*pudor*), though it does not dislodge from the mind the purity (*pudicitia*) maintained so steadfastly."[15] *Pudicia* and *pudor* have a common foundation in the Sanskrit root *pu*,[16] meaning the two words have an intimate connection with each other. Augustine uses this connection, drawing attention to the feeling of shame (*pudor)* that can lead women who possess chastity (*pudicitia*) to suicide. For Augustine, *pudor* seems to have been a keyword in his conception of human beings' sin. In his commentary on Genesis, he explains that what Adam hid with a fig leaf was *pudor.*[17] And in the *Confessiones*, as Virginia Burrus points out, *pudor* appears in the vivid passages in which Augustine depicts his own inner state.[18] Augustine recognizes that he himself, like every human being since Adam's sin, bears this sin in his own mind—the sin he had labeled in Lucretia's mind with the phrase "*pudoris infirmitas.*"

Augustine does not deny that Lucretia held *pudicia*, in that he believes Lucretia did not consent to the assault. He also asks, "as for those who in this situation killed themselves to avoid any suffering of this kind, would anyone with human feeling refuse to pardon them?"[19] He does not jeer at the pagan woman. His aim in discussing the motivation of Lucretia's suicide is to demonstrate the contrast between the way pagan women think and the way Christian women think. Contrary to Lucretia, according to Augustine, Christian women "possess the inner glory of chastity (*castitas*) as witness to their innocence; they possess it before the eyes of their God, and they require nothing more."[20] Augustine focuses on the difference between the Roman woman who worries about people's opinion and loves earthly honor, and (Roman) Christian women who are satisfied with being in God's eye. He begins this discussion saying that "we are more concerned to comfort our own people rather than to provide an answer for outsiders." And the book itself, *De civitate dei*, was written against pagans. But when we pay attention to his recognition that the feeling of shame is often engendered in victims of rape, we may be able to discern an intention to comfort and encourage not only Christian victims. Augustine might also be trying to show pagan victims that Christianity has a way of thinking that allows the victim to find a way to live even after their assault.[21]

---

14 Harper 2013, 173.

15 De civ. D. 1.16.

16 Pellauer 1995, 212.

17 For example, De Genesi ad litteram, 11.32.42; 33.44; 34.46.

18 Conf. 8.7.18. See Burrus 2013, 38-46.

19 De civ. D. 1.17.

20 De civ. D. 1.19. "abent quippe intus gloriam castitatis, testimonium conscientiae; habent autem coram oculis Dei sui nec requirunt amblius..."

21 "No philosopher prior to Augustine had ever taken note of rape as an occasion warranting consolation, i.e., as an experience that occasions grief and requires encouragement and support in

### *Pudicitia* and *sanctitas*

In Augustine's discussion about women who were raped, not only "*pudicitia*" but also "*castitas*" can be translated as "chastity." The difference between these two words is ambiguous in Augustine's usage. Both words are used to refer to both Lucretia and Christian women, but "*pudicitia*" is ascribed mainly to Lucretia. This is understandable because, as Kate Wilkinson says, *pudicitia* is a "common term throughout the (ancient Roman) literature" when referring to the womanly virtue of modesty.[22] Another virtue Augustine mentions here as one women should have is "*sanctitas*," used only in reference to Christian women. "*Sanctitas* (*sanctus*, *sanctifico* etc.)" is appears in many verses of the Bible, with the meaning of purity or an uninjured state.[23] As *pudicitia* (and *castitas*) also include the meaning of purity, Augustine relates them to one another closely:

> Chastity (*pudicitia*) is a virtue of mind, and its companion is the courage which enables it to endure any evils whatsoever rather than to have truck with evil. … if it (*pudicitia*) is a good of the mind, it is not lost even when the body is taken by force. Indeed, when the good of holy continence (*sanctae continentiae bonum*) refuses to yield to the impiety of carnal lusts, the body too is sanctified. So when it perseveres with unbroken resolve in not yielding to those lusts, holiness (*sanctitas*) does not quit the body itself, because the will continues to deploy it in a holy way (*sancte*), as also does the ability to act, in so far as the body allows. For the holiness of the body (*corpus sanctum*) does not lie in the fact that its parts remain undamaged, … I do not think that anyone is so asinine as to believe that the girl lost any of her bodily holiness (*sanctitas*), though her maidenhead (*integritas*) had now been breached. … the holiness (*sanctitas*) of the body is not lost while the holiness (*sanctitas*) of the mind remains, even if the body has been violated.[24]

Augustine employs the expression "*sanctae continentiae bonum*" as the explanation of the concept of *pudicitia* switches to the argument about the *sanctitas* of women's bodies. Although *pudicitia* is used in various meanings, Augustine focuses on the meaning

order that the survivor might continue to live with the dignity that characterized her life prior to the loss." (Webb 2013, 57.)

22 Wilkinson 2015, 14-15.

23 See "ἅγιος" in Von Balz und Schneider 1992.

24 De civ. D. 1.18. (Walsh 2005, 59-60.) "pudicitia virtus sit animi comitemque habeat fortitudinem, qua potius quaelibet mala tolerare quam malo consentire decernit, … Si autem animi bonum est, etiam oppresso corpore non amittitur. Quin etiam sanctae continentiae bonum cum immunditiae carnalium concupiscentiarum non cedit, et ipsum corpus sanctificatur, et ideo, cum eis non cedere inconcussa intentione persistit, nec de ipso corpore perit sanctitas, quia eo sancte utendi perseverat voluntas et, quantum est in ipso, etiam facultas. Neque enim eo corpus sanctum est, quod eius membra sunt integra, … Non opinor quemquam tam stulte sapere, ut huic perisse aliquid existimet etiam de ipsius corporis sanctitate, quamvis membri illius integritate iam perdita. … non amitti corporis sanctitatem manente animi sanctitate etiam corpore oppresso…"

of purity. And, in this discussion, this purity is especially about sexual desire. Thus, *continentia*, a kind of power of abstinence from desires, has a meaning close to *pudicia* here. Augustine adds the adjective "*sancta*" to "*continentia*," thus ingeniously shifting to the argument about how women can keep their purity intact with reference to the religious word "*sanctitas*."

Some regard the uninjured state of parts of the body as testimony to a woman's bodily sanctity, namely virginity, even today. Augustine denies this idea, as we saw in the above quotation. He distinguishes sanctity/holiness (*sanctitas*) of body from its integrity (*integritas*). As for integrity, it can be lost from a body, whatever the state of mind is. Yet sanctity, according to Augustine, will not be lost from a body if the mind is holy. Since the loss of bodily sanctity only occurs if lust is experienced in the body, this body is interpreted as a sense organ. It can be said that Augustine differentiates between the body as a physical being, and the body as a sensory being, which feels pleasures. The former state of being is held in common with inanimate objects like stones, and the latter state is held in common with animals. In the second book of his *De libero arbitrio*, Augustine discusses a hierarchy of being, that is, physical body, sense (external sense, inner sense), reason, and god.[25] The lower components in this hierarchy should obey the higher ones. This hierarchy reflects on the discussion of the sanctity of body and mind in *De civitate Dei*, in that he says there that the sanctity of mind reflects on the sanctity of body. The sanctity of mind is love toward God. Lucretia, whose love was not turned toward God, did not possess purity as *sanctitas*, even if she possessed purity as *pudicitia*. For Augustine, purity means possessing not only *pudicitia* but also *sanctitia*.

By this shift of focus from *pudicitia* to *sanctitas*, the state of desire in the body necessarily becomes the focal point. Some scholars disagree with Augustine's assumption that a victim of rape may sometimes experience sexual desire when they are raped. These scholars claim that "rape is the opposite of pleasurable for the victims,"[26] and "most are frightened and hurt, fearing that they will be killed in the course of the assault."[27] Augustine's assumption is imprudent, but it is important to note that his argument is radically based on the concept of hierarchy of being, and thus it is imaginable for Augustine that a body would feel lust when the mind, the body's governor, lacks perfect control; the power of mind is perfect in no human being after Adam's sin. We should remember how deeply he laments his weakness, which cannot control lusts perfectly, in his *Confessiones*.[28] We should also remember that he was engaged in debate with Pelagianism when he wrote the first book of *De civitate Dei*. In the Pelagian controversy, Augustine emphasizes the weakness of will that every human being has, refuting the Pelagians' opinion that stresses the ability of will to choose goodness. His

25 De libero arbitrio 2.3.7-2.15.40.

26 Miles 2012, 80.

27 Pellauer 1995, 216.

28 Conf. 10.30.41-10.41.66.

assumption that some victims of rape may experience lust is spoken with an empathy that comes from his own experience of the uncontrollable state of his own desires.[29]

### *Corpus* and *animus*

Augustine defines lust in *De libero arbitrio* as "a love that one may lose unwillingly."[30] The objects of lust are temporal things. In contrast, when one loves eternal existence, one lives well, and the eternal existence is God. In the same book, Augustine notes that, regarding the hierarchy of being, one who possesses a higher component of this hierarchy also has all of the lower components; thus, loving God includes loving one's own body and mind. When loving one's body is necessary to loving God, the body itself is not regarded as bad, although lust occurs in the body. This understanding of body certainly seems to be different from Platonism, whose negative view of the body had an effect on the younger Augustine. Is there a change in Augustine's conception of the body? His idea of the hierarchy of being was originally from Greek philosophy or Porphyry, and his argument about suicide is based on Platonic ontology.[31] The noteworthy point here is that, as we saw above, Augustine argues that if one possesses the sanctity of the mind, one possesses the sanctity of the body as well. He goes beyond the hierarchy of being, to find an intimate relationship between these two components of body and mind. Augustine does not regard body as a thing that should be surpassed; for him, it can be purified by purity of mind.[32] This intimate relationship is concerned with sanctity. Lucretia was not regarded as having sanctity because she did not love God. It is clear, then, that Augustine also applies the order of love to that hierarchy of being. Using the order of love, Augustine allows for the possibility of purifying the body. He does not change his concept of the body itself, but deepens his understanding of the relationship between body and mind.

The idea that the sanctity of the mind reflects on the sanctity of the body seems to have succeeded in consoling victims of rape, in that it means a victim's body can keep its purity when they love God. No one can defile others' bodies. Some may think that this idea can be beneficial to victims in modern times, too. In conclusion, however, I would like to address another of Augustine's discussions of rape,[33] which seems to be based on the same idea of the relationship between body and mind:

---

29 Though he is still open to criticism for underestimating the difference between a victim of rape and himself.

30 De libero arbitrio 1.4.10. In De mendacio 7.10, it is said that "lust itself is defined as an appetite of the mind by which certain temporal goods are set before eternal goods." English translation by Muldowney in Muldowney et al. 1952.

31 See Sato 2015.

32 This relationship can be called a "harmony," as Hunter says. See Hunter 2012, 360.

33 Augustine's defined rape in this/the context of this argument as "whatever violence the body suffers without the individual's consent to lust (quod violenter non praecedente libidine patitur corpus)." (De mendacio 7.10.)

> To some persons, bodily chastity (*pudicitia*) seems of such honorable character that it may demand the telling of a lie and that the lie should be told without hesitation if, by means of it, a person attacking one with evil intent may be thwarted. The answer to this problem can be given readily: There is no chastity of the body unless it derives from the integrity of the soul. When the integrity of the soul has been violated, that of the body necessarily collapses even though it may appear intact; on that account, bodily chastity is not to be numbered among temporal things as if it could be taken away against one's wishes. In no way, therefore, should the soul defile itself by a lie for the sake of its body, because of this realization that the body remains incorrupt if innocence does not depart from the soul itself.[34]

This is a text from *De mendacio*, which was written in 395. Augustine, who states his opinion here as an answer to a general question, uses not *sanctitas* but *pudicitia*, a word that commonly refers to the chastity of a rape victim. It is noteworthy that Augustine suggests here, too, that the chastity of the mind reflects on the chastity of body. Telling a lie is an act against the truth. As God is the truth, telling a lie defiles the chastity of mind. Chastity of mind should take precedence over chastity of body; if the former is lost, then so is the latter. Therefore, Augustine insists, no one should tell a lie, even if by lying they could defend their own body from suffering. Those who disagree with his opinion may say that such an act is suicidal – but Augustine would answer that even if you were killed, all you would lose would be temporal life; if you were to tell a lie, you would lose your eternal life. If one tries to be honest and is killed as a result, one becomes a kind of martyr. Augustine's understanding of the relationship between body and mind regarding their purity, which is the basis of the first book of *De civitate Dei* about Lucretia and Christian rape victims, seems to position sufferers between consolation and martyrdom.

## Conclusion

As mentioned above, Augustine is sometimes criticized by modern scholars because he blames Lucretia for killing herself after her rape, and also examines the possibility that a victim of rape might experience sexual desire in the midst of suffering. Augustine may be seen as an unenlightened perpetrator of victim-blaming. Similarly, his severe proclamation about lying may be seen as unrealistic. The gulf between Augustine's attitudes and our own seems insurmountable. However, as confirmed above, Augustine

---

34 De mendacio 7.10. "Pudicitia quippe corporis, quia multum honorabili persona videtur occurrere, et pro se flagitare mendacium, ut si stuprator irruat qui possit mendacio devitari, sine dubitatione mentiendum sit: facile responderi potest, nullam esse pudicitiam corporis, nisi ab integritate animi pendeat; qua disrupta cadat necesse est, etiamsi intacta videatur; et ideo non in rebus temporalibus esse numerandam, quasi quae invitis possit auferri. Nullo modo igitur animus se mendacio corrumpit pro corpore suo, quod scit manere incorruptum, si ab ipso animo incorruptio non recedat."

does not intend to blame Lucretia as a pagan; the aim of his argument is rather to show another way of thinking that allows the victim to live on after their suffering. This way of thinking was different not only from the pagans but also from other Christian authors of his time.[35] Augustine finds a way to keep one's body and mind pure in loving God. The difficulty of this is a big problem for Augustine himself. His recognition of the difficulty of controlling his own desires is reflected in his argument about victims of rape. His position is not set out by drawing lines between "us Christians" or "us men," and "pagans" or "women." He writes that anyone who does not live in the eternal life with perfect love toward God, is the like a traveler who wavers between a wrong path and the right one.

Finally let me mention the title of this paper. In his discussion about the relationship of body and mind, Augustine always uses the words *corpus* and *animus*. *Animus* is usually translated as "mind." Muldowney, however, the English translator of *De mendacio* whom I quote, translates *animus* as "soul,"; "body and mind" might be more suitable for this paper's title. In the same discussions, Augustine mentions *anima* as well, and in each instance, the meaning is close to "life." As we saw, his discussion of rape is intimately related to his understanding of temporal life and eternal life. If the purification or sanctification of body and mind happens, then people gain eternal life, where they live with perfect love. I cannot say why I feel a deeper kind of love is present in the expression "body and soul," as opposed to "body and mind," but regardless, it is clear that Augustine tries to encourage people to love God with a deeper, ideally perfect love – that is, loving with their "body and soul," just like the title of the song.

---

35 See n.10.

# A FLUIDITY OF CANON AND TEXTUAL CRITICISM IN THE WORKS OF ORIGEN

ANNA USACHEVA

**ABSTRACT** *There are two distinct scholarly views on Origen's practice of textual criticism. Bruce Metzger has suggested that Origen was remarkably indifferent towards the key aspects of classical textual criticism and never aimed to create a formal critical edition of the Bible (1963). John McGuckin argued that Origen followed the tradition of Homeric scholarship, pursuing work on a textus criticus of the Bible (2003). I challenge both positions by showing that although Origen applied the methodology of Alexandrian philologists, he never omitted spurious biblical readings. Instead, his Hexapla represented a comprehensive edition of the Bible. Origen's careful approach to biblical texts can be also seen in his dealings with the canon. Although he took part in canonical debates, he did not create a proper list of the authoritative books of Scripture. To understand these seemingly puzzling principles of Origen's biblical studies I turn to textual fluidity and other aspects of manuscript culture, which necessitate revisiting our modern view of ancient canonical thinking, as well as the modern phenomenon of decanonization.*

## Introduction

In recent scholarship the phenomenon of the canon of Scripture has attracted a great deal of scholarly attention.[1] One of the trends in these discussions is the concept of decanonization.[2] In his presentation at the international conference *Canonization and Decanonization*, organized by the Leiden Institute for the Study of Religions in 1997, H. M. Vos defined decanonization as the deconstruction of "that which once was considered to form a unity".[3] He argues that a process of decanonization resulted from historical-critical analysis of the Bible initiated by believing Christians, emphasizing that "the very inquiry into the essence of the canon can actually operate to destroy the canon. In this way the canon falls victim to its own pretension".[4]

According to this logic, a canon is synonymous with a limitation of freedom. It is established by an authoritative community and is valid as long as this community

1 An informative overview of contemporary discussion on the issue can be found in the 662-page collection of essays The Canon Debate, edited by Lee Martin McDonald and James A. Sanders (2002).

2 A comprehensive analysis of recent discussions may be found in an essay anthology edited by Eve-Marie Becker and Susanne Scholz (2011).

3 Cf. Vos 1998, 363.

4 Ibid.

maintains its power.[5] Thus, Vos claims that "freedom of mind and de-canonization go hand in hand because it is this very freedom which stands at odds with the demand that the Bible, by prerogative, must be the directive and standard for the spiritual life".[6]

Although I find it appropriate to talk about the process of decanonization as a modern phenomenon, I would nevertheless like to suggest a more flexible vision of the ancient canon. It seems misleading to see canonization as homogeneous, that is, to assume different authors at different times understood and treated it similarly. For one thing, the modern mindset is framed by the printing press culture, in which the ideas of text, publication, and authorship are different from the reading and writing practices of the manuscript culture. I suggest that these differences should be taken into account in the canon debate. In this article I go back to the end of the second and the beginning of the third century CE, when for various reasons the discussion about the canon of Scripture first appeared in a Christian context. The focus is on Origen, his principles of textual criticism, and his conceptions of text and the canon.

### Canonical thinking in Origen's works

In the mid-second century Marcion provoked a discussion about the canon of Scripture, and particularly about the authoritative books of the New Testament. In the third century, Origen actively argued against Marcion's practice of rejecting spurious fragments in the Bible.[7] He invested a lot of time in studying the Septuagint and the New Testament literature. Despite all his achievements in biblical studies and his active participation in canonical debates, we do not have any evidence to suggest that Origen established any list of the authoritative books of the New Testament. In the fourth century, Eusebius gave a condensed account of Origen's canonical views. He reported that Origen argued for the canonicity of the four gospels according to Matthew, Mark, Luke, and John; he doubted the second epistle of Peter, the three epistles of John, and the Book of Revelation (*HE* 6.25). As for the Epistle to the Hebrews, Origen admitted its canonicity but claimed that "who wrote this epistle, in truth, God knows" (*HE* 6.25). This conclusion shows that apostolic authorship was not a compulsory criterion for his positive decision about the authoritative status of the text.

As for the Old Testament canon, Eusebius tells us that Origen accepted the twenty-two canonical books of the Old Testament "as the Hebrews have handed them down

5 Another contributor to the conference Canonization and Decanonization, H. J. Adriaanse, maintained: "Canons are historically conditioned things; as a matter of fact, they have their epoch of preparation, their epoch of being established – canonization in the proper sense – their epoch of being operative, their epoch of disintegration and invalidation and, finally, their pluperfect, the epoch of their complete disappearance." (cf. Adriaanse 1998, 315).

6 Cf. Vos 1998, 367.

7 Cf. Orig. Comm. in Jn. 5.7.1–2: "an apostolic saying not understood by the followers of Marcion, who therefore athetize the Gospels (ἀθετούντων τά εὐαγγέλια)". Cf. also Orig. Comm. in Jn. 5.7.1–2.

corresponding with the number of their letters" (*HE* 6.25). This shows that Origen did not take credit for establishing a list of authoritative books of the Old Testament, but simply transmitted one of the existing traditions.[8] Thus, in his *Letter to Africanus* Origen reported that he took part in debate on the canonicity of the Book of Daniel. Africanus doubted the authenticity of the story of Susanna, which he considered a "modern composition and a forgery (σύγγραμμα νεωτερικὸν καὶ πεπλασμένον)" because of its fine phrases, "which not even Philistion the play-writer would have used".[9] Interestingly, Origen agreed with Africanus about the fine phrasing of Susanna's story, but he still refused to believe that it was a forgery. Instead, Origen suspected that it "was concealed and removed from the Scriptures by men themselves not very far removed from the counsel of these elders".[10]

This evidence shows, perhaps surprisingly, that Origen was both deeply involved in debating the authoritative status of the biblical books and uninterested in creating a fixed and closed canon of the Holy Scripture, as was done by Athanasius in 367.[11]

This observation leads us to question the objectives of Origen's biblical studies. Of course, we cannot say whether or not the creation of a fixed canon of the New Testament was ever on Origen's agenda, but it is safe to say that it was definitely not among his most pressing issues. Instead, what really piqued his scholarly concern was a problem of discrepancy between the biblical manuscripts. In other words, I believe that the real motive of Origen's studies was not what books should be in the canon, but rather what texts should be in the books of the Old and New Testaments. Origen expounds the underlying purpose of his studies in his *Letter to Africanus*:

> What need is there to speak of Exodus, where there is such diversity (ἐπὶ πολὺ παρήλλακται) in what is said about the tabernacle and its court, and the ark, and the garments of the high priest and the priests, that sometimes the meaning even does not seem to be akin (ὡς μηδὲ τὴν διάνοιαν παραπλησίαν εἶναι δοκεῖν)?[12]

In his *Commentary on Matthew*, Origen reported that "large differences between the manuscripts (τῶν ἀντιγράφων διαφορά)" resulted either from the negligence or from the perverse boldness of some copyists, who "either neglect to check over what they have transcribed, or, in the process of checking, they make additions or deletions as they please (ἀπὸ τῶν τά ἑαυτοῖς δοκοῦντα ἐν τῇ διορθώσει <ἢ> προστιθέντων ἢ ἀφαιρούντων)."[13]

---

8 An overview of the discussions around the Old Testament canon can be found in Barton 2013, 145-164.

9 Ep. ad Afr. 49.15.

10 Ep. ad Afr. 11.69.15.

11 In his Easter Letter (Ep. 39), Athanasius gives a list of authoritative books that he recommended for reading in Egyptian churches. He claimed that no one should add or take away any of the books on this list (cf. Metzger 1987, 135-141).

12 Ep. ad Afr. 11.57.1.

13 Comm. in Matth. 15.14. Transl. Metzger 1963, 78-79.

Notoriously, these significant differences between the biblical manuscripts created a serious research problem in terms of choosing between various readings. Yet even this problem was not half as vexing as the puzzling oddities which sprang from discrepancies between the Hebrew and Greek languages. Origen describes this stylistic discrepancy in the *Letter to Africanus*, where he points to "the so-called etymological fancies, which in the Hebrew are perfectly suitable, but not in the Greek (οἱονεὶ ἐτυμολογίαι αἵτινες παρά μὲν Ἑβραίοις οἰκείως ἔχουσι, παρά δὲ ἡμῖν οὐχ ὁμοίως)".[14] Origen affirms that some of the biblical solecisms found in the Septuagint sprang from loose or even fallacious translations.[15]

Presented with these research problems, Origen, an heir of both the Hellenic and the Jewish Alexandrian traditions, first tried to solve them by means of philological (grammatical) analysis. From the *Commentary on John* we learn that some of the earlier Jewish and Christian scholars were likewise committed to meticulous grammatical studies and engaged in the textual criticism of biblical manuscripts.[16] They investigated the style and grammar of the Greek translations of the Bible in order to detect pseudepigrapha and textual forgery in the biblical texts. Like many of his predecessors and contemporaries, Origen was deeply engaged in textual criticism and grammatical studies of biblical texts. In these circumstances, it seems natural that establishing the biblical canon was not among his major goals. Instead, he devoted his attention to clearing up discrepancies between the manuscripts, which logically should precede evaluating the texts.

Besides, if we take into account the manuscript culture of the second and third centuries CE, it becomes clear that the practical impact of the official canonization of certain biblical books could not possibly have been as straightforward and influential as someone more familiar with printing press culture might expect. Living in the printing press universe, we can easily imagine how church or governmental authorities control the publication of the Bible. In a manuscript culture where books were copied by hand and were very expensive, the majority of Christians simply could not afford to own a full edition of the Bible. Although increasing popularity of the codex primed thinking about which books were included in a biblical edition, it was not until the fourth century that the development of binding technology allowed the creation of such comprehensive editions of the Bible as Sinaiticus and Vaticanus.[17] In these circumstances, when production of the comprehensive editions of the Bible was exceedingly expensive and very rare, any canonical decision of the church naturally lost one half of its effectiveness. Instead of functioning as an instrument of church control over the

14 Ep. ad Afr. 11.76.55.

15 Cf. Orig. Ep. ad Afr. 77.25: "For in many other passages we can find traces of this kind of contrivance (οἰκονομικῶς τινα) on the part of the translators, which I noticed when I was collating the various editions (συνεξετάζοντες πάσας τάς ἐκδόσεις ἀλλήλαις)."

16 Cf. Orig. Comm. in Jn. 6.40.204: "We are not unaware that 'these things were done in Bethania' occurs in nearly all the manuscripts. It seems likely too that, in addition, this was the earlier reading. And, to be sure, we have read 'Bethania' in Heracleon."

17 Cf. Kloppenborg 2014, 22.

publication of the Bible, the canon functions rather as a recommendation to Christian readers. Another feature of the manuscript culture is textual variations, which called for meticulous philological analysis.

In his article "Origen as literary critic in the Alexandrian tradition", J.-A. McGuckin argues that Origen trod in the steps of Alexandrian textual critiques by aiming at creating a *textus criticus* of the Bible. Although I agree with McGuckin's thesis about Origen's expertise in Alexandrian textual criticism, I do not agree that his goal was a *textus criticus*. Earlier, Bruce Metzger had claimed that Origen never attempted to prepare a formal edition of the New Testament. I am inclined to accept Metzger's conclusion, though I feel uneasy about his critique of Origen's "remarkable indifference to what are now regarded as important aspects of textual criticism".[18] Origen was obviously well-versed in classical textual criticism, and he applied the typical Aristarchian signs (asterisk and obelisk) to mark textual differences between manuscripts.[19] Given the extent of Origen's practical engagement with textual criticism of the Bible, it would be odd to claim his indifference towards this subject. However, he explicitly stated in his *Commentary on Matthew* that he did not dare to remove the passages that he found were subjects of disagreement between the Hebrew and Greek manuscripts. This practice of keeping the spurious fragments in the text is different from the omission of readings which are very weakly attested in the manuscripts, as practised by Alexandrian Homeric scholars. For instance, Aristarchus allowed omission of readings, although he often explained his position in ὑπομνήματα.[20] While Origen rejected omission, I do not see this as a token of his indifference to text-critical techniques, but rather as an attempt to adjust the rules of textual criticism to Christian scripture. Thus, instead of omitting spurious readings Origen suggested adding to the Septuagint some new passages from the Hebrew Bible:

> For the lack of consistency in the manuscripts of the Old Testament, we have with God's help found a cure, while we use the remaining manuscripts as a yardstick; what was dubious in the Septuagint on account of manuscripts lacking consistency, we judge this from the rest of the manuscripts, and retain whatever is in harmony. Moreover, such places that are missing from the Hebrew text we mark with an obelisk ([because] we do not dare to erase them completely). Other places we mark with an asterisk to make clear that what we added is not found in the Septuagint, but is found in the Hebrew and some manuscripts [of the Septuagint].

18 Metzer 1963, 95.

19 To give one short example, in the Fragments from the Commentary on John Origen tells about the Jews, who silently assumed (κατά τὸ σιωπώμενον, Comm. in Jn., fr. 77.14) that Christ could be identified with a Samaritan. This passage suggests that Origen was familiar with Aristarchus' κατά τὸ σιωπώμενον technique, that is to say, a practice of making silent assumptions from the text (Schol. Il. 21.17a).

20 Cf. Nagy 1998, online.

Whoever wants can accept these variants, but to whom this is objectionable, can either accept or refuse depending on his judgement.[21]

The last sentence of this passage is especially remarkable. By stating that the reader may feel free either to accept or to reject his suggested variant readings, Origen provided the Christian exegete with unprecedented research freedom. His rather liberal view of biblical studies and humble approach to the results of his research appear to be at odds with what we might expect from a scholar who devoted his life to biblical studies. I believe that the reason Origen held back from making final judgements about the biblical manuscripts was not his humility or lack of self-confidence, but his engagement with the practice of biblical studies, which he considered a kind of spiritual exercise. He meticulously recorded all extant readings, no matter how wild they seemed at first blush. His reasoning is clear:

Nay, I suppose that every letter, no matter how strange, which is written in the oracles of God, does its work (ἀλλγάρ οἶμαι ὅτι καὶ πᾶν θαυμάσιον γράμμα τὸ γεγραμμένον ἐν τοῖς λογίοις τοῦ θεοῦ ἐργάζεται).[22]

Origen insisted upon studying variant readings not for the sake of reconstructing the original text (as was the purpose of the Homeric scholars and those Jewish scholars who followed their path), nor for the sake of preserving a canonized version of a sacred text (as was the common pursuit of conservative Jewish exegetes[23]), but for the sake of a deep and multifarious understanding of the biblical text and its transmission history directed by Providence.[24]

### Classical Homeric Scholarship and Origen's Textual Criticism

In an attempt to trace the background of Origen's biblical studies, I shall now return to classical scholarship, where the foundational ideas for Alexandrian textual criticism were first aired. In his seminal *Aporemata Homerica*, Aristotle introduced the practice of multiple solutions of textual contradictions. The general structure of the Aristotelian study of Homeric questions consisted of the following elements: the contradictory frag-

---

21 Comm. in Matt. 15.14.

22 Comm. in Jer. fr. 2.1 = Philoc. 10.1.

23 The accounts of a conservative reaction that some Alexandrian Jews showed to the biblical textual criticism and of their conviction in the sacral status of the LXX is preserved in the Letter of Aristeas 310-11, Aristobulus' Questions and Answers, preserved in Eusebius' Praeparatio evangelica (cf., e.g., Praep. evang. 8.10.6), and Philo's Allegorical Commentary and Questions and Answers on Genesis and Exodus, which are generally concerned with explaining the puzzling fragments of the LXX and confirming the sacred status of the translation. (Cf. Niehoff 2011, 20-23, 71, 152-58).

24 A compelling testimony of Origen's devotion to manuscript studies is given by Eusebius, who in his Historia Ecclesiastica tells us that Origen found unknown manuscripts of Psalms in a jar in Jericho, which he embedded in his Hexapla (HE 6.16.3). A description of Origen's Hexapla is preserved in Jerome's Commentary on Epistle to Titus 3.9 (PL 26, 734d–735a), and Eusebius' Church History (HE 6.16).

ment, the δι τί inquiry about it, and a few possible solutions to the issue. In chapter 25 of the *Poetics* Aristotle justifies the multiplicity of possible answers by pointing to the multivocality of being:

> With regard to problems, and the various solutions of them, how many kinds there are, and the nature of each kind, all will be clear if we look at them like this. Since the poet represents life, as a painter does or any other maker of likenesses, he must always represent one of three things — either things as they were or are (οἷα ἦν ἢ ἔστιν); or things as they are said and seem to be (οἷά φασιν καὶ δοκεῖ); or things as they should be (οἷα εἶναι δεῖ).[25]

Similarly, Origen in his *De Principiis* contends:

> Scripture interweaves the imaginative with the historical, sometimes introducing what is utterly impossible (πῆ μὲν μηδὲ δυνατὸν γενέσθαι), sometimes what is possible but has never occurred (πῆ δὲ δυνατὸν μὲν γενέσθαι, οὐ μὴν γεγενημένον).[26]

Aristotle applied different logical, grammatical, historical, and stylistic arguments in order to solve textual puzzles. If all these arguments failed to provide consistency in a given questionable fragment, he assumed that the author had for some reason applied dramatic effect in the text. Homeric scholars, Jewish exegetes, and Origen also explained particularly troublesome fragments by assuming deliberate authorial usage of dramatic effect.[27] Porphyry informs us that Aristarchus elaborated the methodology of justification of textual contradictions by suggesting a comparison of parallel fragments.[28] Thus, for Aristarchus a seemingly nonsensical phrase (τὸ ἀδύνατον) can be clarified, justified, and understood through comparison with another context or reading. Aristarchus used this technique in his running commentaries and also as the main instrument for the emendation of Homeric text, namely when he transferred some passages into different contexts, under the pretext that "this line is not properly placed here".[29]

Origen also searched for and compared parallel fragments of the Bible in order to understand their inner logic and various individual levels of meaning:

---

25 Poet. 1460b5–11.

26 De Princ. 4.2.9 = Philoc. 1.16. Here and later the translation of the Philocalia fragments is from G. Lewis 1911 (available online).

27 On the whole, Origen stood with Philo and Aristotle, who supposed that the authoritative text (of the Bible or of Homer) was free from any inconsistency and that each and every questionable fragment could be justified by a meticulous scholar (cf. Or., Philoc. 9.30).

28 Although Aristarchus' authorship of the famous dictum "αὐτὸς μὲν ἑαυτὸν πολλὰ Ὅμηρος ἐξηγεῖται" preserved by Porphyry is questionable (Porph., HQ 1.1.12f.), the method of comparison of parallel readings assuredly goes back to Aristarchus (in support of this idea cf. Eustathios, Il. 2.101.14f.).

29 Schol. Il. 1.177a.

the only way to begin to understand the Scriptures is (οὐκ ἄλλοθεν τάς ἀφορμάς τοῦ νοεῖσθαι λαμβανούσας) by means of other passages containing the explanation dispersed throughout them (ἢ παρ' ἀλλήλων ἐχουσῶν ἐν αὐταῖς διεσπαρμένον τὸ ἐξηγητικόν).[30]

Yet Origen sought for parallel readings not only throughout Scripture but also in certain relevant passages of the most authoritative classical compositions. Thus, he significantly broadened the background of Scripture and allowed readers of holy texts to grasp the contextual framework of biblical concepts and notions.[31] Although he applied classical contexts only for the sake of interpretation and never equated their authority with the authority of biblical texts, nonetheless Origen's readerly horizon was exceedingly broad and comprehensive.

In order to outline the bedrock principles of Origen's biblical studies, I would like to pinpoint certain passages from the *Philocalia*.

1. Origen forbade emendation of the solecistic phrases of Scripture. The entire eighth chapter of the *Philocalia*, excerpted from the *Commentary on Hosea*, is devoted to this topic and is correspondingly titled:

   That we need not attempt to correct the solecistic phrases of Scripture. (Περὶ τοῦ μὴ δεῖν τά σολοικοειδῆ ῥητά τῆς γραφῆς ἐπιχειρεῖν διορθοῦσθαι).[32]

2. Origen also forbade the rejection of spurious fragments, arguing that rejecting fragments of Scripture was heretical. Here are his thoughts on this issue in his *Commentary on Hezekiah*:

   There are some who err in respect of the Gospel pasture and the apostolic water, so that they tread down certain portions of the Gospel field and feed on others as on good pasture, either rejecting the whole apostolic pasture, or approving some parts and rejecting others. Let us feed on the whole of the Gospels and not tread down any part of them (ἁμαρτανόντων δέ τινων καὶ περὶ τὴν εὐαγγελικὴν νομὴν καὶ τὸ ἀποστολικὸν ὕδωρ, ὥστε τῶν εὐαγγελικῶν τινά μὲν πατεῖν τινά δὲ ὡς καλὴν νέμεσθαι νομὴν, καὶ τῶν ἀποστολικῶν ἢ πάντα ἀποκρίνειν, ἤ τινα μὲν

30 Cf. Orig., Sel. in Ps., PG XII 1080.37 = Philocalia 2.3.

31 In such a way, Origen did not restrict himself to explaining the Bible only by referring to the Bible itself, but often employed classical philosophy. For instance, in the Commentary on John (2.93), Origen in order to prove that evil is "nothing" and was not created by God, referred to the Platonic understanding of "nothingness" and "non being" familiar from the Parmenides 130c: "And as certain Greeks say that the genus and species, such as living being and man, belong to the category of "no things," so they have supposed "nothing" to be everything which has received its apparent constitution neither from God nor through the Word". (transl. Heine 1989, 118-119).

32 Philoc. 8.1n.

ἐγκρίνειν τινά δὲ ἀποκρίνειν, ἡμεῖς καὶ τά ὅλα Εὐαγγέλια νεμηθῶμεν, καὶ μηδὲν αὐτῶν πατήσωμεν).[33]

3. Origen acknowledged that not all readings are of equal authenticity and that certain readings might indeed be fallacious. Yet, interestingly enough, this did not prevent him from stating together with the apostle Paul that this variety of readings is only natural and even reasonable because, as the Apostle asserted:

   No doubt there have to be differences among you to show which of you have God's approval (Δεῖ γάρ καὶ αἱρέσεις ἐν ὑμῖν εἶναι, ἵνα οἱ δόκιμοι φανεροὶ γένωνται ἐν ὑμῖν [1 Cor 11:19]).[34]

4. In sum, these complementary principles elucidate Origen's vision of biblical studies, whose aim, as I emphasized earlier, consists in acquiring a comprehensive vision of biblical readings in both the Hebrew and the Greek traditions, which allows the exegete to penetrate a multi-dimensional and universal divine message. Origen conceded that acquiring such a comprehensive vision required an ascetic way of life, which may or may not bring the scholar to a desirable result (for only saints, after all, are able to penetrate the divine message). He thus asserted:

   The saint is a sort of spiritual herbalist, who culls from the sacred Scriptures every jot and every common letter, discovers the value of what is written and its use, and finds that there is nothing superfluous in the Scriptures (οὕτως οἱονεὶ βοτανικός τις πνευματικός ἐστιν ὁ ἅγιος, ἀναλεγόμενος ἀπὸ τῶν ἱερῶν γραμμάτων ἕκαστον ἰῶτα καὶ ἕκαστον τὸ τυχὸν στοιχεῖον, καὶ εὑρίσκων τὴν δύναμιν τοῦ γράμματος, καὶ εἰς ὅτι ἐστὶ χρήσιμον, καὶ ὅτι οὐδὲν παρέλκει τῶν γεγραμμένων).[35]

These principles of biblical studies were set out in the *Hexapla*, which represented a ground-breaking methodological and technical innovation in Hellenic philology. It is important, however, to recognize the heavy methodological baggage that emerged together with the composition of *Hexapla*.[36] What distinguishes Origen's approach from the textual criticism of Hellenic and Jewish scholars is a pioneering and outstandingly high estimation of various *receptions* of the text. Whilst admitting that the Greek versions of Aquila and Symmachus had some forgeries deliberately inserted by the Jews, he neither emended nor rejected these versions from his collection.[37] These versions were

---

33 Comm. in Ezech., fr. 13.665.5 = Philoc. 11.2.

34 C. Cels. 3.13.2 = Philoc. 16.2.

35 Comm. in Jer., fr. 2.2 = Philoc. 10.2.

36 For details about Hexapla's methodological innovation cf. Grafton and Williams 2006, 104f.

37 For instance, Origen argued that Jews, in order to reject the story of Susanna and many other narratives and passages accepted in Christian tradition, "introduced some phrases manifestly incorrect (λέξεις τινάς τάς μὴ πρεπούσας παρεμβεβληκότων τῇ γραφῇ)" (Ep. ad Afr. 11.65.25).

important for him because they shed light on the Jewish tradition of the reception of the Bible, which he employed in his Hexapla project.[38]

Although Origen knew that a commonly accepted version of the Bible would contribute to peace in the Church, he would not forego the opportunity to study variant readings preserved in different manuscripts. He recommended some readings as authoritative and others as spurious but never rejected them entirely. In the context of the Hellenic reading and writing culture, such a flexible approach to the text was not extraordinary. For instance, it is attested in modern biblical scholarship that the New Testament manuscript culture was characterized by so-called textual fluidity.[39] It is in the same vein that, with a reference to Bernard Cerquiglini's *Éloge de la variante*, Hugo Lundhaug, who studies monastic manuscript culture in late antique Egypt,[40] assumes that manuscript variants should not be considered a deviation from the norm but a natural product of scribal culture, where the textual variant represented the norm.[41]

In a recent article Matthew Larsen challenged the traditional conception of New Testament textual criticism by taking a closer look at some previously overlooked aspects of ancient writing practices and textual fluidity. He argued that:

> The prevalence of accidental publication, stolen texts and author variants simultaneously identifies and destabilizes one of the foundational assumptions of traditional textual criticism: without the assumption of a text existing in a final form, the boundaries between text, form and redaction criticism fall apart.[42]

The idea of a canon is closely connected to and even depends upon the idea of text. Consequently, there is a difference between the canonical thinking of a manuscript culture, which is characterized by textual fluidity, and the canonical thinking of the culture of a publishing press. In the circumstances of textual fluidity, Origen could hardly consider variant readings as a necessary evil. He was deeply engulfed in studies of the transmission of the biblical texts, and compiling a fixed list of authoritative books was less important to him than the unlimited study of Scripture. And after all, in the absence of the printing press, it was difficult to control the production and dissemination of biblical editions. Thus, the ancient editions of the Bible were characterized by

38 Cf. Com. in Matth. 15.14 cited above, where Origen tells about his practice of marking out the passages in the LXX that are not found in the Hebrew Bible. Another testimony to Origen's interest in the Jewish tradition of the reception of the Bible is that in the Commentary on John (2.87). Origen explicitly refers to the Gospel according to the Hebrews, which he cites in order to confirm his argument. On the Jewish-Christian character of the Gospel of the Hebrews cf.: Schneemelcher and Wilson 2003, 173.

39 Cf. the details about the history of the concept in Lundhaug and Lied 2017, 1.

40 An ERC-financed research project New Contexts for Old Texts: Unorthodox Texts and Monastic Manuscript Culture in Fourth- and Fifth-Century Egypt (NEWCONT), directed by Professor Hugo Lundhaug (University of Oslo).

41 Cf. Lundhaug 2017, 2; Cerquiglini 1999, 77f.

42 Cf. Larsen 2017, 376.

numerous variant readings and differences in the list and sequence of the books.[43] For centuries after Origen, authoritative Christian authors disagreed about including or excluding certain texts in the biblical canon, and admittedly their disagreements did not split the church.[44]

## Conclusion

In conclusion, I would like to recall the modern views on the phenomenon of the canon cited at the beginning of this article. Some contemporary scholars have commented on the de-canonization that was provoked by the rigid and indisputable status of the biblical canon that previously dominated the Christian church. I do not wish to doubt this conclusion, but to challenge its rigidity. As shown in this article, in the Early Church, both the biblical texts and the list of authoritative books were rather fluid. In these circumstances, Origen encouraged Christian exegetes to study the transmission history of biblical texts instead of attempting a reconstruction of the original version of the text. Many later Christian authors highly valued Origen's scholarly opinion. Besides, a genuine interest in biblical studies inspired many exegetes after Origen to address questions of the authorship and status of spurious texts in the canon. This fact allows for flexibility in dealing with such complex notions as the canon and canonization. The proclamation of certain lists of authoritative books by the councils did not preclude members of the church either from reading and copying spurious and non-authoritative books, or from questioning the status of the authoritative books.[45] Before the invention of the printing press the accuracy of the editions of the Bible was in the hands of scribes who left us with numerous variant readings and variations in listing, structuring, and layout of the textual material. After the invention of the printing press Lutheran biblical scholarship challenged the previous traditional canonical thinking; since then the investigation and questioning of biblical literature have never ceased.

Regarding the contemporary phenomenon of decanonization, it would be more profitable to consider such notions as the canon and canonization in connection with the reading, writing, and publishing culture of Late Antiquity. After all, Bible editions depend not only on the decisions of church institutions but also on reading and writing technologies, on the practical means of the publication process, and also on the persons in charge of this enterprise. These aspects of biblical textuality should be taken into account in modern discussions of the phenomenon of the canon.

43 Cf. Parcer 2013, 430-436.

44 Cf. Metzger 1987, 209-218.

45 In the appendices to The Canon Debate, McDonald gives the prescribed lists of the Early Christian canons of the Old and New Testaments (McDonald 2002, 585-597).

# BIBLIOGRAPHY

## Aeschylus' Persians: Empathizing with the Enemy, or Orientalizing Them?


Abulafia, D. (ed.) 2003. *The Mediterranean in History*. London: Thames and Hudson.

Anderson, B. 1991. *Imagined Communities. Reflections on the Origins and Spread of Nationalism*. Second edition. London – New York: Verso.

Archibald, Z. H. 2013. *Ancient Economies of the Northern Aegean. Fifth to First Centuries BC*. Oxford: Oxford University Press.

Bakewell, G. 1997. Review of Hall 1996, *Bryn Mawr Classical Review*, 13 August.

Braudel, F. 1966[2]. *La Méditerranée et le monde méditerranéen à l'époque de Philippe II*. Paris: Colin (first edn Paris 1949).

Bridges, E., E. Hall, and P. Rhodes (eds) 2008. *Cultural Responses to the Greek Wars. Antiquity to the Third Millennium*. Oxford: Oxford University Press.

Browning, R. 2002. "Greeks and Others. From Antiquity to Renaissance", in Harrison 2012, 257-277.

Burian, P. 1997. "Myth into *Muthos*: the Shaping of the Tragic Plot", in P. E. Easterling (ed.), *The Cambridge Companion to Greek Tragedy*, Cambridge: Cambridge University Press, 178-208.

Burkert, W. 1992. *The Orientalizing Revolution*. Cambridge: Cambridge University Press.

Cartledge, P. 1993. *The Greeks. Portrait of Self and Other*. Cambridge: Cambridge University Press.

Cartledge, P. 2009. *Ancient Greek Political Thought in Practice*. Cambridge: Cambridge University Press.

Derks, T. and N. Roymans (eds.) 2009. *Ethnic Constructs in Antiquity. The Role of Power and Tradition*. Amsterdam: Amsterdam University Press.

Duthat, R. 2016. "The Myth of Cosmopolitanism", *The New York Times*, 2 July. (www.nytimes.com/2016/07/03/opinion/sunday/the-myth-of-cosmopolitanism.html?_r=1)

Easterling, P. E. 1987. "Notes on Tragedy and Epic", in L. Rodley, *Papers Given at a Colloquium on Greek Drama in Honour of R. P. Winnington-Ingram*), London: Hell. Soc. Supp. 15, 52-61.

Garvie, A. F. (ed.) 2009. *Aeschylus. Persae, with Introduction and Commentary*. Oxford: Oxford University Press.

Giordano, M. 1999. *La supplica. Rituale, istituzione sociale e tema epico*. Naples: Quaderni di *AION*.

Giordano, M. 2013. "*Alien wisdom*: il viaggio di *sophia*", in A. Ercolani and P. Xella (eds), *La Sapienza nel Vicino Oriente e nel Mediterraneo antichi*, Rome: Carocci, 19-42.

Giordano, M. 2016. "The emergence of Athens", in A. Ercolani and M. Giordano, M. (eds), *Submerged Literature. Comparative and Anthropological perspectives*, Berlin and Boston: de Gruyter, 55-70.

Giordano forthcoming, *The Emergence of Athens: War Tragedy, and Identity (477-467 BCE)*.

Goldhill, S. 1988. "Battle Narrative and Politics in Aeschylus' *Persae*", *JHS* 108: 189-193.

Gruen, E. S. (ed.) 2011. *Cultural Identity in the Ancient Mediterranean*. Los Angeles: Getty Research Institute.

Hall, E. 1989. *Inventing the Barbarian. Greek Self-definition Through Tragedy*. Oxford: Oxford University Press.

Hall, E. 1996. *Aeschylus Persians* (Comm.). Warminster: Aris and Phillips.

Hall, J. M. 1997. *Ethnic Identity in Greek Antiquity*. Cambridge: Cambridge University Press.

Hall, J. M. 2009. "Polis, Community, and Ethnic Identity", in H. A. Shapiro (ed.), *The Cambridge Companion to Archaic Greece*, Cambridge: Cambridge University Press, 40-60.

Harrison, Th. 2000. *The Emptiness of Asia. Aeschylus' Persians and the History of the Fifth Century*. London: Duckworth.

Harrison, Th. 2002. *Greeks and Barbarians*. Edinburgh: Edinburgh University Press.

Herman, G. 1987. *Guest-Friendship and the Greek City*. Cambridge: Cambridge University Press.

Horden, P. and N. Purcell 2000. *The Corrupting Sea. A Study of Mediterranean History*. Oxford: Blackwell.

Hornblower, S. 2008. "Greek Identity in the Archaic and Classical Periods", in K. Zacharia (ed.), *Hellenism. Culture, Identity, and Ethnicity from Antiquity to Modernity*, London: Routledge, 37-58.

Luce, J. M. (éd.) 2006. *Identités ethniques dans le monde Grec Antique* (Actes du Colloque Toulouse 2006). Toulouse: Presse Universitaire du Mirail.

Malkin, I. 1998. *The Returns of Odysseus. Colonization and Ethnicity*. Berkeley and Los Angeles: University of California Press.

Malkin, I. 2001. *Ancient Perceptions of Greek Ethnicity*. Cambridge (Mass.) – London: Harvard University Press.

Malkin, I. (ed.) 2005. *Mediterranean Paradigms and Classical Antiquity*. London – New York: Routledge.

Malkin, I. 2005a. "Networks and the Emergence of Greek Identity", in Malkin 2005, 56-74.

Malkin, I., C. Constantakopoulos, and K. Panagopoulou (eds.) 2009. *Greek and Roman Networks in the Mediterranean*. London and New York: Routledge.

Morris, I. 2005. "Mediterraneanization", in Malkin 2005, 30-55.

McInerney, J. (ed.) 2014. *A Companion to Ethnicity in the Ancient Mediterranean.* Malden – MA – Oxford: Wiley-Blackwell.

Murray, A. T. 1924. *Homer. The Iliad*, with an English translation by A.T. Murray, vol. 2. London: Heinemann (Loeb Classical Library).

Murray, G. 1940, *Aeschylus. The Creator of Tragedy*. Oxford: Oxford University Press.

Miller, M.C. 1997. *Athens and Persia in the Fifth Century BC. A Study in Cultural Receptivity*. Cambridge: Cambridge University Press.

Osborne, R. 2012. "Landscape, Ethnicity, and the Polis", in Stoddart and Cifani 2012, 24-31.

Oudemans, Th. C. W. and A. P. M. H. Ladinois 1987. *Tragic Ambiguity. Anthropology, Philosophy and Sophocles' Antigone*. Leiden: Brill.

Petropoulos, E. K. 2006. Review of Irad Malkin 2005, *Bryn Mawr Classical Review*, 4 February.

Raaflaub, K. 2009. "Learning from the Enemy: Athenian and Persian 'Instruments of Empire'", in J. Ma, N. Papazarkadas, R. and Parker (eds.), *Interpreting the Athenian Empire*, Oxford: Oxford University Press, 89-124.

Rollinger, R. 2006. "The Eastern Mediterranean and Beyond: The Relations between the Worlds of the "Greek" and "Non-Greek" Civilizations', in K. H. Kitzl (ed.), *A Companion to the Classical Greek World*, Malden Ma and Oxford: Wiley-Blackwell, 197-226.

Said, E. 1978. *Orientalism*. New York: Vintage Books Editions.

Stoddart, S. and G. Cifani 2012. *Landscape, Ethnicity and Identity in the Archaic Mediterranean Area*. Oxford: Oxbow Books.

Stoddart, S. and G. Cifani 2012. "Introduction. Contextualizing Ethnicity", in Stoddart and Cifani 2012, 1-4.

Weir Smyth, H. 1930. *Aeschylus. Volume 1: Suppliant Maidens, Persians, Prometheus, Seven Against Thebes*, translated by Herbert Weir Smyth. London: Heinemann (Loeb Classical Library).

### Revelation at the Limit: Mystery and Matter after the Valentinians

Anaxagoras of Clezomenae. 2010. *Fragments and Testimonia*. Translated with commentary by Patricia Curd. Toronto: University of Toronto Press.

Anonymous. 1997. *Liber Viginti Quattuor Philosophorum*. Translated by Markus Vinzent. Turnhout: Brepols.

Aristotle. 1933. *Metaphysics*. Translated by Hugh Tredennick. London: William Heinemann Ltd.

Aristotle. 2008. *Physics*. Translated by Robin Waterfield. Oxford: Oxford University Press.

Aristoxenus. 1902. *The Harmonics of Aristoxenus (Elementa Harmonia)*. Translated by Henry S. Macran. Oxford: Clarendon Press.

Attridge, H. W. (ed.) 1985. *Nag Hammadi Codex I: The Jung Codex* Leiden: Brill.

Augustine. 2003. *City of God*. Translated by Henry Bettenson. New York: Penguin.

Bennett, Jane. 2001. *The Enchantment of Modern Life: Attachments, Crossings, and Ethics*. Princeton, NJ: Princeton University Press.

Braidotti, Rosi. 2000. "Teratologies", in Ian Buchanan and Claire Colebrook (eds), *Deleuze and Feminism*, Edinburgh: Edinburgh University Press, 156-72.

Brakke, David. 2009. "The Body as/ At the Boundary of Gnosis", *Journal of Early Christian Studies* 17/2: 195-215.

Brons, David. Undated a. "Christ and the Church". http://gnosis.org/library/valentinus/Christ_and_Church.htm. Accessed April 26, 2017.

Brons, David. Undated b. "The Name and Naming in Valentinianism". http://gnosis.org/library/valentinus/Name_Naming.htm. Accessed April 26, 2017.

Brons, David. Undated c. "Realized Eschatology". http://gnosis.org/library/valentinus/Realized_Eschatology.htm. Accessed April 26, 2017.

Brons, David. Undated d. "Valentinian Theology". http://gnosis.org/library/valentinus/Valentinian_Theology.htm. Accessed April 27, 2017.

Bryant, Levi. 2014. *Onto-Cartography: An Ontology of Machines and Media*. Edinburgh: Edinburgh University Press.

Clement of Alexandria. 1934. *Excerpts of Theodotus (Excerpta Ex Theodoto)*. Translated by Robert Pierce Casey. London: Christophers.

Craig, Ryann E. 2012. "Anastasis in the Treatise on the Resurection: What Jesus' Resurrection Teaches About Valentinian Christology", in G. van Oyen and T. Shepherd (eds), *Resurrection of the Dead: Biblical Traditions in Dialogue*, Leuven: Peeters, 475-96.

DeLanda, Manuel. 1995. "A Geology of Morals: A Neo-Materialist Interpretation". Presented at *Virtual Futures 95*.

Diogenes Laëtius. 2014. *Lives and Opinions of Eminent Philosophers, Including the Biographies of the Cynics and the Life of Epicurus*. Translated by Robert Drew Hicks. New York: Gottfried and Fritz.

Dolphijn, Rick and Iris van der Tuin (eds) 2012. *New Materialisms: Interviews and Cartographies*. Ann Arbor, MI: Open Humanities Press (An imprint of Michigan Publishing, University of Michigan Library).

Frost, Diana and Samantha Coole (eds) 2010. *New Materialisms: Ontology, Agency, and Politics*. Durham, NC: Duke University Press.

Funk, Wolf-Peter (translator) 2007. "The First Revelation of James", in Marvin Meyer (ed.), *The Nag Hammadi Scriptures*, New York: HarperCollins, 321-32.

Harman, Graham. 2010. "Object-Oriented Philosophy (1999)", in *Towards Speculative Realism*, Hants, UK: Zero Books, 93-104.

Hippolytus. 1886. *The Refutation of All Heresies*. Translated by J. H. MacMahon. Buffalo, NY: Christian Literature Publishing.

Irenaeus. 1992. *Against the Heresies Volume 1*. Translated by Dominic J. Unger, with Further Revisions by John J. Dillon. New York: The Newman Press.

Keller, Catherine and Mary-Jane Rubenstein (eds) 2017. *Entangled Worlds: Religion, Science, and New Materialisms*. New York: Fordham University Press.

Layton, Bentley (translator) 1987. "The Gospel According to Philip", in Bentley Layton (ed.), *The Gnostic Scriptures*, New York: Doubleday, 329-53.

Layton, Bentley (translator) 1987. "The Gospel of Truth", in Bentley Layton (ed.), *Gnostic Scriptures*, New York: Doubleday, 253-64.

Lehtipuu, Outi. 2015. *Debates Over the Resurrection of the Dead: Constructing Early Christian Identity*. Oxford: Oxford University Press.

Miller, Mitchell. 1995. "The Choice Between the Dialogues and the 'Unwritten Teachings': A Scylla and Charybdis for the Interpreter?", in Francisco Gonzalez (ed.), *The Third Way: New Directions in Platonic Studies*, Lanham, MD: Rowman and Littlefield, 225-44.

Pearson, Birger A. (translator) 2007. "The Teachings of Silvanus,", in Marvin Meyer (ed.), *The Nag Hammadi Scriptures*, New York: HarperCollins, 499-521.

Plato. 1996. *Apology*. Translated by Harold North Fowler. London: William Heinemann.

Plato. 1996. *Parmenides*. Translated by Albert Keith Whitaker. Newburyport, MA: Focus Publishing.

Plato. 1993. *Philebus*. Translated by Dorothea Frede. Indianapolis, IN: Hackett Publishing.

Plato. 1995. *Phaedrus*. Translated by Alexander Nehamas and Paul Woodruff. Indianapolis, IN: Hackett Publishing.

Plato. 2008. *The Republic*. Translated by Robin Waterfield. Oxford: Oxford University Press.

Plato. 1995. *The Statesman*. Translated by Robin Waterfield. Cambridge, UK: Cambridge University Press.

Plato. 1989. *The Symposium*. Translated by Alexander Nehemas and Paul Woodruff. Indianapolis, IN: Hackett Publishing.

Plato. 2014. *Theaetetus*. Translated by John McDowell. Oxford: Oxford University Press.

Sayre, Kenneth. 1983. *Plato's Late Ontology: A Riddle Resolved*. Princeton, NJ: Princeton University Press.

Tertullian. 2016. *On the Resurrection*. Translated by Ernest Evans. Eugene, OR: Wipf and Stock.

Theophrastus. 2010. *On First Principles (Known as His Metaphysics)*. Translated by D. Gutas. Leiden: Brill.

Thomassen, Einar. 1980. "The Structure of the Transcendent World in the Tripartite Tractate (Nhc I, 5)", *Vigilae Chrsitianae* 34: 358-75.

Thomassen, Einar, and Marvin Meyer (translators) 2007. "A Valentinian Exposition", in Marvin Meyer (ed.), *The Nag Hammadi Scriptures*, New York: HarperCollins, 663-79.

Thomassen, Einar (translator) 2007. "The Tripartite Tractate", in Marvin Meyer (ed.), *The Nag Hammadi Scriptures*, New York: HarperCollins, 57-101.

Turner, John D. (translator). Undated. "The Allogenes: Annotated Edition including Line Numbers)," in *The Nag Hammadi Library Online*. http://gnosis.org/naghamm/allogenes-jdt-ln.html. Accessed March 23, 2019.

## Decolonizing Ancient Sexuality: Three Case Studies

Armour, E. T. and S. M. St Ville (eds.) 2006. *Bodily Citations: Religion and Judith Butler*. New York: Columbia University Press.

Atkinson, Ti-Grace. 1974. *Amazon Odyssey*. New York: Link Books.

Blondell, R. and K. Ormand (eds.) 2015. *Ancient Sex: New Essays*. Columbus: Ohio State University Press.

Boyarin, D. 1998. "Gender", in Taylor 1998, 117-135.

Butler, J. 1995. "Contingent Foundations: Feminism and the Question of 'Postmodernism'", in *Feminist Contentions: A Philosophical Exchange*, New York: Routledge, 35-57.

Cahana, J. 2016. "Gnosticism and Radical Feminism: From Pathologizing Submersion to Salvaging Re-Emergence", in Ercolani and Giordano 2016, 183-200.

Cahana-Blum, J. 2018. *Wrestling with Archons: Gnosticism as a Critical Theory of Culture*. Lanham, MD: Lexington Books.

Dworkin, A. 1987. *Intercourse*. New York: The Free Press.

Edelman, Lee. 2004. *No Future: Queer Theory and the Death Drive*. Durham: Duke University Press.

Ercolani, A. and M. Giordano (eds.) 2016. *Submerged Literature in Ancient Greek Culture: The Comparative Perspective*. Berlin: De Gruyter.

Halperin, David. 1990. *One Hundred Years of Homosexuality*. New York: Routledge.

Halperin, David. 2015. "Not Fade Away", in Blondell and Ormand 2015, 308-328.

Latour, B. 1993. *We Have Never Been Modern*. Cambridge: Harvard University Press.

Laqueur, T. 1990. *Making Sex: Body and Gender from the Greeks to Freud*. Cambridge: Harvard University Press.

Laqueur, T. 2003. "Sex in the Flesh", *Isis* 94: 300-306.

Martin, D. B. 2006. *Sex and the Single Savior: Gender and Sexuality in Biblical Interpretation*. Louisville: Westminster John Knox Press.

Millet, Kate. 2000. *Sexual Politics*. Chicago: University of Illinois Press.

Sha, Richard. 2006. "The Uses and Abuses of Historicism: Halperin and Shelley on the Otherness of Ancient Greek Sexuality", in *Historicizing Romantic Sexuality (Romantic Circles Praxis)*, online: http://www.rc.umd.edu/praxis/sexuality/sha/sha.html

Stone, Ken. 2006. "The Garden of Eden and the Heterosexual Contract", in Armour and St Ville 2006, 48-70.

Taylor, M. (ed.) 1998. *Critical Terms for Religious Studies*. Chicago: University of Chicago Press.

## Myths as 'Cultural Vectors': Some reflections on Ancient Greece and Modern Ethnographic Traditions

Assmann, J. 1988. "Kollektive Gedächtnis und kulturelle Identität", in Assmann and Hölscher 1988: 9-19.

Assmann, J. 1992. *Das Kulturelle Gedächtnis: Schrift, Erinnerung und politische Identität in frühen Hochkulturen*. Munich: Verlag C. H. Beck.

Assmann, J. 2006. *Religion and Cultural Memory. Ten Studies*. Stanford – CA: Stanford University Press.

Assmann, J. and T. Hölscher (eds) 1988. *Kultur und Gedächtnis*. Frankfurt am Main: Suhrkamp.

Bettini, M. 2016. *Radici. Tradizione, identità, memoria*. Bologna: Il Mulino.

Bianchi Bandinelli, R. (ed.) 1989. *Storia e civiltà die Greci*. Vol. I. Milano: Bompiani.

Bierl, A. 2015. "New Trends in Homeric Scholarship (NTHS)", in Latacz, Bierl, and Olson 2015, 177-203.

Billings, J. 2014. Genealogy of the Tragic: Greek Tragedy and German Philosophy. Princeton and Oxford: Princeton University Press.

Breglia, L., A. Moleti, and M. L. Napolitano (a cura di) 2011. *Ethne, identità e tradizioni: la "terza" Grecia e l'Occidente*. Pisa: Edizioni ETS.

Brillante, C. 1990. "Myth and History. History and the Historical Interpretation of Myth", in Edmunds 1990, 91-138.

Buxton, R. 1994. *Imaginary Greece. The context of mythology*. Cambridge: Cambridge University Press.

Buxton, R. (ed.) 1999. *From Myth to Reason? Studies in the Development of Greek Thought*. Oxford: Oxford University Press.

Calame, C. 2011. *Poetiche dei miti in Grecia antica*. Lecce: Argo.

Calame, C. 2015. *Qu'est-ce que la mythologie grecque?*, Paris: Gallimard.

Calame, C. and B. Lincoln (par) 2012. *Comparer en histoire de religions antiques. Controverses et propositions.* Liège: Presses Universitaires de Liège.

Cambiano, G., L. Canfora, and D. Lanza (a cura di) 1992. *Lo spazio letterario della Grecia antica,* I. *La produzione e la circolazione del testo.* 1. *La polis.* Roma: Salerno Editrice.

Casadio, G. 2009. "Mythos *vs* Mito. Mythos *vs* Myth", *Minerva* 22: 41-63.

Cerri, G. 1986a. "Lo statuto del guerriero morto nel diritto della guerra omerica e la novità del libro XXIV dell'*Iliade* – Teoria dell'oralità e storia del testo", in Cerri 1986, 1-53.

Cerri, G. (a cura di) 1986. *Scrivere e recitare. Modelli di trasmissione del testo poetico nell'antichità e nel medioevo.* Atti di una ricerca interdisciplinare svolta presso l'I.U.O. Roma: Edizioni dell'Ateneo.

Colesanti, G. and M. Giordano (eds) 2014. *Submerged Literature in Ancient Greek Culture. An Introduction.* Berlin – Boston: De Gruyter.

Defradas, J. 1954. *Les thèmes de la propagande delphique.* Paris: Librairie C. Klincksiek.

Dei, F. 2015. "Il mito in Malinowski e nell'antropologia Britannica", in Leghissa and Manera 2015, 81-90.

Detienne, M. 1981. *L'invention de la mythologie.* Paris: Éditions Gallimard.

Detienne, M. 2005. *Les Grecs and nous.* Paris: Éditions Perrin.

Detienne, M. 2009. *Comparer l'incomparable.* Paris: Éditions du Seuil.

DeWalt, K. M. and B. R. DeWalt (eds) 2011. *Participant Observation. A Guide for Fieldworkers.* Lanham – New York – Toronto – Plymouth (UK): Altamira Press.

Dowden, K. and N. Livingstone (eds) 2011. *A Companion to Greek Mythology.* Malden (MA) – Oxford: Wiley – Blackwell.

Duret-Pujol, M. (sous la direction de) 2016. *Comique et politique chez le Modernes et les Anciens* (*Artes* 13). Bordeaux: Presses Universitaires de Bordeaux.

Edmunds, L. 1990. *Approaches to Greek Myth.* Baltimore: Johns Hopkins University Press.

Ercolani, A. 2014. "Defining the Indefinable: Greek Submerged Literature and Some Problems of Terminology", in Colesanti and Giordano 2014, 7-18.

Ercolani, A. and M. Giordano (eds) 2016. *Submerged Literature in Ancient Greek Culture. The Comparative Perspective.* Berlin – Boston: De Gruyter.

Erll, A. 2011. *Memory in Culture.* London: Palgrave – Macmillan.

Erll, A. and A. Nünning (eds) 2008. *Cultural Memory Studies. An International and Interdisciplinary Handbook.* Berlin – New York: Walter de Gruyter.

Firth, R. 1960a. "Introduction: Malinowski as Scientist and as Man", in Firth 1960, 1-14.

Firth, R. (ed.) 1960b (?). *Man and Culture. An Evaluation of the Work of Bronislaw Malinowski.* London: Routledge & Kegan Paul.

Fowler, R. L. 2011. "*Mythos* and *Logos*", *JHS* 131: 45-66.

Fowler, R. L. 2016. "The Submersion of Mythography", in Ercolani and Giordano 2016, 43-54.

Fowler, R. L. 2006. "How to Tell a Myth: Genealogy, Mythology, Mythography", *Kernos* 19: 35-46.

Franchi, E. and G. Proietti (a cura di) 2012. *Forme della memoria e dinamiche identitarie nell'antichità greco-romana.* Trento: Università degli Studi di Trento.

Gentili, B. 2006. *Poesia e pubblico nella Grecia antica. Da Omero al V secolo.* Milano: Feltrinelli.

Gernet, L. 2004. *Polyvalences des images. Testi e frammenti sulla leggenda greca.* Editi da A. Soldani, Pisa: ETS.

Giordano, M. 2004. "*Edipo a Colono:* la palinodia della colpa", *SemRom* 7/2: 183-205.

Giordano, M. 2005. "As Socrates Shows, the Athenians Did Not Believe in Gods", *Numen* 52/3: 325-355.

Giordano, M. 2006. "Ritual Appropriateness in *Seven against Thebes.* Civic Religion in a Time of War", *Mnemosyne* 59/1: 53-74.

Graf, F. 2011. "Myth and Hellenic Identities", in Dowden and Livingstone 2011, 211-226.

Halbwachs, M. 1950. *La mémoire collective.* Paris: Presses Universitaires de France.

Hawes, G. 2014a. *Rationalizing Myth in Antiquity.* Oxford: Oxford University Press.

Hawes, G. 2014b. "Story Time at the Library: Palaephatus and the Emergence of Highly Literate Mythology", in Scodel 2014, 125-147.

Hobsbawm, E. J. and T. Range (eds) 1983. *The Invention of Tradition.* Cambridge: Cambridge University Press.

Jensen, J. S. (ed.) 2009. *Myth and Mythologies. A Reader.* London: Equinox.

Kindt, J. 2012. *Rethinking Greek Religion.* Cambridge: Cambridge University Press.

Korzybski, A. 1933. "A Non-Aristotelian System and its Necessity for Rigour in Mathematics and Physics", in Korzybski 1933a, 747-761.

Korzybski, A. 1933a. *Science and Sanity: An Introduction to Non-Aristotelian Systems and General Semantics*. Lakelville, CT: International Non-Aristotelian Library.

Latacz, J., A. Bierl, and S. D. Olson (eds) 2015. *Homer's Iliad. The Basel Commentary. Prolegomena*. Berlin – Boston: De Gruyter 2015.

Leghissa, G. and E. Manera (a cura di) 2015. *Filosofia del mito nel Novecento*. Roma: Carocci.

Lesky, A. 1939. "Orestes", *RE* 18/1: 966-1010.

Lincoln, B. 1999. *Theorizing Myth. Narrative, Ideology, and Scholarship*. Chicago: University of Chicago Press.

López Eire, A. and M. del H. Velasco López 2012. *La mitología griega: lenguaje de dioses y hombres*, Madrid: Arco/Libros.

Malinowski, B. 1921. "Ethnology and the Study of Society", *Economica* 2: 208-219.

Malinowski, B. 2002 [1922]. *Argonauts of the Western Pacific*. London: Routledge.

Malinowski, B. 1923. "Psycho-analysis and Anthropology", *Nature* 112: 650-651 [reprinted in *Sex, Culture and Myth*. New York City: Harcourt, Brace & World 1962, 114-116].

Malinowski, B. 1926. *Myth in Primitive Psychology*. New York: Norton & Co. [reprinted in *Magic, Science and Religion and Other Essays*. Glencoe, Illinois: The Free Press 1948, 72-124].

Malinowski, B. 1927a. *Sex and Repression in Savage Society*. London: Routledge & Kegan Paul.

Malinowski, B. 1927b. "Obscenity and Myth", in Malinowski 1927, 104-134.

Malinowski, B. 1936. *The Foundations of Faiths and Morals*. Oxford: Oxford University Press [reprinted in Malinowski 1962, 295-336].

Malinowski, B. 1962a. *Sex, Culture, and Myth*. New York: Harcourt, Brace & World.

Malinowski, B. 1962b. "Myth as a Dramatic Development of Dogma", in Malinowski 1962a (?), 245-265.

Mele, A. 2011. "Oreste a Metauros", in Breglia, Moleti, and Napolitano 2011, 353-371.

Montanari, E., A. Rengakos, and Ch. Tsagalis (eds) 2012. *Homeric Contexts. Neoanalysis and the Interpretation of Oral Poetry*. Berlin – Boston: De Gruyter.

Morgan, K. 2000. *Myth and Philosophy from the Presocratics to Plato*. Cambridge: Cambridge University Press.

Müller, K. O. 1991 [1825]. *Prolegomeni ad una mitologia scientifica*. Napoli: Guida.

Murray, O. and S. Price (eds) 1990. *The Greek City from Homer to Alexander*. Oxford: Calderon Press.

Oudemans, Th. C. W. and A. P. M. H. Lardinois 1987. *Tragic Ambiguity. Anthropology, Philosophy and Sophocles' Antigone*. Leiden – New York – København – Köln: E. J. Brill.

Palmisciano, R. 2014. "Submerged Literature in an Oral Culture", in Colesanti and Giordano 2014, 19-32.

Parker, R. 2011. *On Greek Religion*. Ithaca (New York): Cornell University.

Pébarthe, C. 2016. "Quand la comparaison est raison ou de l'intérêt de comparer les Anciens et les Modernes" 2, in Duret-Pujol 2016, 247-274.

Pirenne-Delforge, V. 2008. *Retour à la source. Pausanias et la religion grecque*. Liège: Presses Universitaires de Liège.

Proietti, G. 2012. "Memoria collettiva e identità etnica. Nuovi programmi teorico-metodologici nella ricerca storica", in Franchi and Proietti 2012, 15-41.

Pucci, L. 2016. "The Purification of Orestes at Troezen: a Case of Submersion between Ancient and Modern", in Ercolani and Giordano 2016, 71-94.

Pucci, L. 2017. *Fuori da Atene. Miti e tradizioni su Oreste in Grecia antica*. Roma: Aracne.

Rossi, L. E. 1989. "I poemi omerici come testimonianza di poesia orale", in Bianchi Bandinelli 1989, 73-147.

Rossi, L. E. 1992. "L'ideologia dell'oralità fino a Platone", in Cambiano, Canfora, and Lanza 1992, 77-106

Schirripa, P. 2010. *Religione e società nella Grecia antica*. Roma: Carocci.

Scodel, R. (ed.) 2014. *Between Orality and Literacy. Communication and Adaptation in Antiquity*. Leiden – Boston: Brill.

Sinding Jensen, J. (ed.) 2009. *Myths and Mythologies. A Reader*. London – Oakville: Equinox.

Sourvinou-Inwood, C. 1988. "Further aspects of polis religion", *AION* (sez. Archeologia) 10: 259-274.

Sourvinou-Inwood, C. 1990. "What is a polis religion?", in Murray and Price 1990, 295-322.

Stocking G. W. Jr. 1986a. "Anthropology and the Science of Irrational. Malinowski' Encounter with Freudian Psychology", in Stocking 1986, 13-49.

Stocking G. W. Jr. (ed.) 1986b (?). *Malinowski, Rivers, Benedict and Others*. Madison – London: The University of Wisconsin Press.

Strenski, I. 1987. *Four Theories of Myth in Twentieth-Century History. Cassirer, Eliade, Lévi-Strauss, and Malinowski.* Iowa City: University of Iowa Press.
Strenski, I. 1992. *Malinowski and the Work of Myth.* Princeton: Princeton University Press.
Thomas, R. 1989. *Oral Tradition and Written Record in Classical Athens.* Cambridge: Cambridge University Press.
Thomas, R. 1992. *Literacy and Orality in Ancient Greece.* Cambridge: Cambridge University Press.
Veyne, P. 1984 [1983]. *I Greci hanno creduto ai loro miti?.* Bologna: Il Mulino.
Vernant, J.-P. 1981 [1974]. *Mito e società nell'antica Grecia. Religione greca, religioni antiche.* Torino: Einaudi.
Woodard, R. D. (ed.) 2007. *The Cambridge Companion to Greek Mythology.* Cambridge: Cambridge University Press.
Young, M. V. 2004. *Malinowski. Odyssey of an Anthropologist, 1884-1920.* New Haven – London: Yale University Press.
Zaidman, L. B. and P. Schmitt-Pantel 1990 [1989]. *La religione greca.* Roma – Bari: Laterza.

## Liberating Levi – A Cultural-Evolutionary Approach to Aramaic and Greek Levi Beyond Denominational Essentialism

Alexander, P. 2006. *The Mystical Texts: Songs of the Sabbath Sacrifice and Related Manuscripts.* London: T&T Clark.
Becker, J. 1970. *Untersuchungen zur Entstehungsgeschichte der Testamente der zwölf Patriarchen.* Leiden: Brill.
Becker, J. 1980. *Die Testamente der zwölf Patriarchen*, JSHRZ 3. Gütersloh: Mohn.
Bellah, R. N. 1964. "Religious Evolution", *American Sociological Review* 29/3: 358-374.
Bellah, R. N. 2005. "What is Axial about the Axial Age?", *Archives of European Sociology* 156/1: 69-87.
Bellah, R. N. and H. Joas (eds) 2012. *The Axial Age and Its Consequences.* Cambridge, MA: Harvard University Press.
Bousset, W. 1900a. "Die Testamente der XII Patriarchen: I. Die Ausschneidung der christlichen Intepretationen", *ZNW* 1: 141-175.
Bousset, W. 1900b. "Die Testamente der XII Patriarchen: II. Composition und Zeit der jüdischen Grundschrift", *ZNW* 1: 187-209.
Boyarin, D. 1997. *A Radical Jew: Paul and the Politics of Identity*, Contraversions: Critical Studies in Jewish Literature, Culture, and Society. Berkeley: University of California Press.
Boyarin, D. 2002. "Justin Martyr Invents Judaism", *Church History* 70: 427-461.
Boyarin, D. 2004. "The Christian Invention of Judaism: The Theodosian Empire and the Rabbinic Refusal of Religion", *Representations* 85/1: 21-57.
Boyarin, D. 2015. *A Traveling Homeland: The Babylonian Talmud as Diaspora.* Pennsylvania: University of Pennsylvania Press.
Boyarin, D. and C. A. Barton 2016. *Imagine No Religion: How Modern Abstractions Hide Ancient Realities.* New York: Fordham University Press.
Braun, F. M. 1960. "Les Testaments des XII Patriarches et le problème de leur origine", *Revue Biblique* 67: 516-549.
Charles, R. H. 1913. *The Apocrypha and Pseudepigrapha of the Old Testament*, vol II (Testaments of the Twelve Patriarchs). Oxford: Clarendon.
Cohen, S. J. D. 1999. *The Beginnings of Jewishness. Boundaries, Varieties, Uncertainties.* Berkeley – Los Angeles – London: University of California Press.
Cohen, S. J. D. and J. J. Schwartz (eds) 2007. *Studies in Josephus and the varieties of ancient Judaism: Louis H. Feldman Jubilee Volume.* Leiden: Brill.
Collins, J. J. 1984. *Apocalyptic Imagination.* New York: Eerdmans.
Daschke, D. 2010. *City of Ruins. Mourning the Destruction of Jerusalem.* Leiden: Brill.
De Jonge, M. 1960. "Christian Influence in the Testaments of the Twelve Patriarchs", *Novum Testamentum* 4: 182-235.
De Jonge, M. 1962. "Once More: Christian Influence in the Testaments of the Twelve Patriarchs", *Novum Testamentum* 5/4: 311-319.
De Jonge, M. 1991. "The Testament of Levi and 'Aramaic Levi'", in *Jewish Eschatology, Early Christian Christology and the Testaments of the Twelve Patriarchs. Collected Essays.* Leiden: Brill, 244-262. De Jonge, M. 1999. "Levi in Aramaic Levi and in the Testament of Levi", in E. G. Chazon and M. E. Stone (eds.), *Pseudepigraphic Perspectives: The Apocrypha and Pseudepigrapha in Light of the Dead Sea Scrolls*, Leiden: Brill, 71-89.
DiTommaso, L. 2001. *A Bibliography of Pseudepigrapha Research 1850-1999.* Sheffield: Sheffield Academic Press.
Eck, Werner (2003). "Hadrian, the Bar Kokhba Revolt, and the Epigraphic Transmission", in P. Schäfer (ed.), *The Bar Kokhba War Reconsidered*, Text and Studies in Ancient Judaism, 100. Tübingen: Mohr Siebeck, 153-170.

Eliav, Y. Z. (2003). "The Urban Layout of Aelia Capitolina: A New View from the Perspective of the Temple Mount", in P. Schäfer (ed.), *The Bar Kokhba War Reconsidered*, Text and Studies in Ancient Judaism, 100. Tübingen: Mohr Siebeck, 241-277.

Feldman, L. H. 1993. *Jew and Gentile in the Ancient World. Attitudes and Interactions from Alexander to Justinian*. Princeton, NJ: Princeton University Press.

Fine, S. (ed.) 2005. *Jews, Christians, and Polytheists in the Ancient Synagogue*. London: Routledge.

Goldstein, E. 2016. "Why I am not fasting on Tisha B'Av", in *Times of Israel*, blog contribution, 04.08.2016, http://blogs.timesofisrael.com/why-im-not-fasting-on-tisha-bav/ (last accessed: 09.11.2016).

Goodman, M. 2004. "Jews proselytising in the first century", in M. Goodman (ed.), *Judaism in the Roman World*. Oxford: Oxford University Press, 91-116.

Goodman, M. 2009. "Religious variety and the Temple in the late Second Temple period and its aftermath", *Journal of Jewish Studies* 60/2: 202-213.

Goodman, M. 2011. "Josephus and variety in first-century Judaism", in J. A. North and S. R. F. Price (eds.), *The Religious History of the Roman Empire: Pagans, Jews and Christians*, Oxford: Oxford University Press, 419-434.

Greenfield, J., M. Stone, and E. Eshel. 2004. *The Aramaic Levi Document: edition, translation, commentary*. Leiden: Brill.

Himmelfarb, M. 2009. "Judaism in antiquity: ethno-religion or national identity", *Jewish Quarterly Review* 99/1: 65-73.

Hultgård, A. 1977, 1981. *L'Eschatologie des Testaments des Douze Patriarches*, 2 vols. Uppsala: Almqvist & Wikseil.

Hunt, T. (2018). "The influence of French colonial humanism on the study of Late Antiquity: Braudel, Marrou, Brown", *International Journal of Francophone Studies* 21/3-4, 255-278.Ilan, T. 2009. "The Torah of the Jews of Rome", *Jewish Studies Quarterly* 16/4: 363-395.

Isaac, B. (2003). "Roman Religious Policy and the Bar Kokhba War", in P. Schäfer (ed.), *The Bar Kokhba War Reconsidered*, Text and Studies in Ancient Judaism, 100. Tübingen: Mohr Siebeck, 37-54.

Fine, S. (ed.) 2005. *Jews, Christians, and Polytheists in the Ancient Synagogue*. London.

Jaspers, K. 1949. *Vom Ursprung und Ziel der Geschichte*. Muenchen.

Johnson, J. 2012. "Trauma and Zion: Narrative Healing", *Lumen et Vita* 2, https://ejournals.bc.edu/ojs/index.php/lumenetvita/article/view/1858 (last accessed: 17.04.2016).

Kee, H. C. 1983. "The Testaments of the Twelve Patriarchs", in R. Charlesworth (ed.), *OTP*, vol. 1, Garden City (NY): Doubleday, 775-828.Klawans, J. 2006. *Purity, Sacrifice, and the Temple. Symbolism and Supersessionism in the Study of Ancient Judaism*. Oxford: Oxford University Press.

Kugel, J. 1993. "Levi's Elevation to the Priesthood in Second Temple Writings", *Harvard Theological Review* 86: 1-64.

Kugler, R. 1996. *From Patriarch to Priest: The Levi-Priestly Tradition from Aramaic Levi to Testament of Levi*, SBL Early Judaism and Its Literature 9. Atlanta: Scholars Press.

Kugler, R. 2001. *The Testaments of the Twelve Patriarchs*. Sheffield: Sheffield Academic Press.

Kugler, R. 2008. "Whose Scripture? Whose Community? Reflections on the Dead Sea Scrolls Then and Now, by Way of Aramaic Levi", *Dead Sea Discoveries* 15: 5-23.

Mason, S. 2007. "Jews, Judaeans, Judaizing, Judaism: Problems of Categorization in Ancient History", *Journal for the Study of Judaism* 38: 457-512.

Mimouni, S. 2015. "Le 'Judaïsme sacerdotal et synagogal" en Palestine et en Diaspora entre le IIe et le VIe siècle: propositions pour un nouveau concept", *CRAI*: 113-147.

Neusner, J. 1985. "Varieties of Judaism in the Formative Age", in A. Green (ed.), *Jewish Spirituality from the Bible through the Middle Ages*. London: SCM, 171-97.

Neusner, J. 1993. *The Way of Torah: An Introduction to Judaism*, 5th ed. Belmont, CA: Wadsworth.

Neusner, J. 2000. *The Emergence of Judaism: Jewish Religion in Response to the Critical Issues of the First Six Centuries*. Lanham, Md.: University Press of America.

Philonenko, M. 1960. *Les interpolations chrétiennes des Testaments des Douze Patriarches et les manuscrits de Qoumrân*. Paris: Presses universitaires de France.

Rajak, T. 2002. "Synagogue and Community in the Graeco-Roman Diaspora", in J. Bartlett (ed.), *Jews in the Hellenistic and Roman Cities*, London: Routledge, 22-38.

Rajak, T. 2014. "Investment in/of the Jerusalem priesthood", in B. Dignas, R. Parker, and G. Stroumsa (eds), *Priests and prophets among Pagans, Jews, and Christians*, Leuven: Peeters, 29-51.

Rüpke, J. and É. Rebillard 2015. *Group Identity and Religious Individuality in Late Antiquity*, CUA Studies in Early Christianity. Washington: Catholic University of America Press.

Rutgers, L. V. 1995. *The Jews in Late Ancient Rome. Evidence of Cultural Interaction in the Roman Diaspora.* Leiden: Brill.

Rutgers, L. V. 2016. "Next Year in Sardis: Reflections on whether the Jewish Diaspora of the Roman Era was Diasporic at all", in C. Cordoni de Gmeinbauer (ed.), *"Let the wise listen and add ot their learning" (Prov. 1:5): Festschrift for Günter Stemberger on the occasion of his 75th birthday*, Berlin: De Gruyter, 167-196.

Sanders, E. P. (ed.) 1981. *Jewish and Christian Self-Definition. Vol. 2. Aspects of Judaism in the Greco-Roman Period.* Philadelphia: Fortress Press.

Satlow, M. 2005. "Disappearing Categories: Using Categories in the Study of Religion", *Method & Theory in the Study of Religion* 17/4: 287-298.

Satlow, M. 2006. "Defining Judaism: Accounting for "Religions" in the Study of Religion", *Journal of the American Academy of Religion* 74/4: 837-860.

Satlow, M. 2008. "Beyond Influence: Toward a New Historiographic Paradigm", in A. Norich and Y. Z. Eliav (eds.), *Jewish Literatures and Cultures: Context and Intertext*, Brown Judaic Studies 349, Providence, R.I.: Brown Judaic Studies, 37-53.

Schäfer, P. (ed.) 2003. *The Bar Kokhba War Reconsidered*, Text and Studies in Ancient Judaism, 100. Tübingen: Mohr Siebeck.

Schäfer, P. 2009. *The Origins of Jewish Mysticism.* Tübingen: Mohr Siebeck.

Sharon, N. 2014. "Roman Conquest and the Loss of Sovereignty", in D. Schwartz and Z. Weiss (eds.), *Was 70 CE a Watershed in Jewish History?*, Leiden: Brill, 415-445.

Slingerland, D. 1977. *The Testaments of the Twelve Patriarchs: A Critical History of Research*, Society of Biblical Literature Monograph Series, 21. Missoula (Montana): Scholars Press.

Smith, J. Z. 1982. *Imagining Religion: From Babylon to Jonestown.* Chicago: University of Chicago Press.

Stewart, B. A. 2015. *Priests of My People. Levitical Paradigms for Early Christian Ministers*, New York: Peter Lang.

Stone, M. 1991. "Ideal Figures and Social Context: Priest and Sage in the Early Second Temple Age", in M. Stone (ed.), *Selected Studies*, SVTP 9, Leiden: Brill, 259-270.

Swartz, M. 2001. "The Dead Sea Scrolls and Later Jewish Magic and Mysticism", *Dead Sea Discoveries* 8: 182-193.

Ulrichsen, J. H. 1991. *Die Grundschrift der Testamente der Zwölf Patriarchen: Eine Untersuchung zu Umfang, Inhalt, und Eigenart der ursprünglichen Schrift.* Stockholm: Almqvist &Wikseil.

Vinzent, M. 2014. *Marcion and the Dating of the Synoptic Gospels.* Leuven: Peeters.

Weil, E. 1975. "What is a breakthrough in history?", *Daedalus* 104/2: 21-36.

Weiss, Z. and D. Schwartz 2014. *Was 70 CE a Watershed in Jewish History?.* Leiden: Brill.

Westeinde, J. van 't 2017. "Sacerdotalisation and early Jewish mystical elements in the Greek *Testament of Levi*", in D. Hamidovic, S. C. Mimouni, and L. Painchaud (eds.), *Les écrits mystiques des Hekhalot et la 'sacerdotalisation' dans le judaïsme ancient, Colloque international à l'Université de Lausanne du 26 au 28 octobre 2015,.* Collection "Judaïsme antique et origines du christianisme", Turnhout: Brepols, in press.

Werman, C. 1997. "Levi and Levites in the Second Temple Period", *Dead Sea Discoveries* 4: 211-225.

### Religion and Politics in the Jewish-Christian War in Sixth-Century Himyar

Attema, D. S. 1949. *Het oudste christendom in Zuid-Arabië.* Amsterdam: Noord-Hollandsche Uitgevers Maatschappij.

Baron, S. W. 1957. *A Social and Religious History of the Jews*, vol. 3. New York: Columbia University Press – Philadelphia: Jewish Publication Society.

Beaucamp, J., F. Briquel-Chatonnet, and C.-J. Robin, C(eds.). 2010. *Juifs et chrétiens en Arabie aux Ve et VIe siècles: Regards croisés sur les sources.* Paris: Centre d'histoire et civilization de Byzance.

Bowersock, G. W. 2013. *The Throne of Adulis: Red Sea Wars on the Eve of Islam.* Oxford: Oxford University Press.

Cook, J. G. 2000. *The Interpretation of the New Testament in Greco-Roman Paganism.* Studien und Texte zu Antike und Christentum 3. Tübingen: Mohr Siebeck.

Detoraki M. and J. Beaucamp. 2007. *Le Martyre de Saint Aréthas et de ses compagnons (BHG 166): édition critique, étude et annotation.* Paris: Association des amis du Centre d'histoire et civilization de Byzance.

Drewes, A. J. 1987. "Ethiopië en Zuid-Arabië tussen 450 en 550 na het begin van onze jaartelling," *Phoenix* 33/1: 55-71.

Gajda, I. 2009. *Le royaume de Himyar à l'époque monothéiste: L'histoire de l'Arabie du sud ancienne de la fin du IVe siècle.* Paris: AIBL & De Boccard.

Gajda, I. 2010. "Quel monothéisme en Arabie du Sud ancienne?," in Beaucamp, Briquel-Chatonnet, and Robin (eds.) 2010, 107-120

Grillmeier, A. 1979. *Jesus Christus im Glauben der Kirche, Band 1: Von der apostolischen Zeit bis zum Konzil von Chalcedon (451)*. Freiburg: Herder.

Guidi, I. 1881. "La lettera di Simeone vescovo di Beth-Arsâm sopra i martiri omeriti," *Atti della Reale Accademia dei Lincei* III: *Memorie della classe dei scienze morali, storiche e filologiche* 7, 471-515.

Guidi, I. 1945. *Raccolta degli scritti I: Oriente cristiano*. Roma: Istituto per l'Oriente.

Hachlili, R. 2001. *The Menorah, the Ancient Seven-Armed Candelabrum: Origin, Form, and Significance*. Supplements to the Journal for the Study of Judaism 68. Leiden: Brill.

Halévy, J. 1889. "Examen critique des sources relatives à la persécution de Nedjran par le roi juif des Himyarites," *Revue des études juives* 18: 16-42 and 161-178.

Hirschberg, H.Z. 1971. "Yusuf 'As'ar Yath'ar Dhu Nuwas," *Encyclopaedia Judaica* 16, 897-900.

Horst, P. W. van der. 2015. *Het joodse koninkrijk van Himyar en de christelijke martelaars van Nadjrân*. Amsterdam: Athenaeum, Polak & Van Gennep.

Jones, A. H. M. and E. Monroe. 2001. *A History of Ethiopia*. Safety Harbor CA: Simon Publications [repr. of the 1935 ed.].

Kobishchanov, Y. M. 1979. *Axum*. University Park – London: Pennsylvania State University Press.

Lahey, L. 2007. "Evidence for Jewish Believers in Christian-Jewish Dialogues through the Sixth Century (Excluding Justin)," in O. Skarsaune and R. Hvalvik (eds.). *Jewish Believers in Jesus*. Peabody: Hendrickson, 581-639

Moberg, A. 1924. *The Book of the Himyarites*. Lund: Gleerup.

Müller, W. W. 1991. "Himyar," *Reallexikon für Antike und Christentum* 15, 303-331.

Newby, G. D. 1988. *History of the Jews of Arabia from Ancient Times to the Eclipse under Islam*. Columbia: University of South Carolina Press.

Robin, C.-J. 2003. "Le judaïsme de Himyar," *Arabia* 1. 97-172.

Robin, C.-J. 2004. "Himyar et Israel," *Comptes rendues de l'Académie des Inscriptions et Belles Lettres* 148. 831-890.

Robin, C.-J. 2008. "Joseph, dernier roi de Himyar (de 522 à 525, ou une des années suivantes)," *Jerusalem Studies in Arabic and Islam* 32. 1-124.

Robin, C.-J. 2010. "Nagrân vers l'époque du massacre: notes sur l'histoire politique, économique et institutionelle et sur l'introduction du christianisme (avec un réexamen du *Martyr d'Azqir*)," in Beaucamp, Briquel-Chatonnet and Robin (eds.) 2010, 39-106.

Ryckmans, J. 1956. *La persécution des chrétiens Himyarites au sixième siècle*. Istanbul: Nederlands historisch-archaeologisch instituut in het Nabije Oosten.

Schäfer, P. 2009. *Jesus in the Talmud*. Princeton: Princeton University Press.

Shahid, I. 1964. "Byzantino-Arabica: The Conference at Ramla, A.D. 524," *Journal of Near Eastern Studies* 23, 115-131.

Shahid, I. 1971. *The Martyrs of Najran: New Documents*. Brussel: Société des Bollandistes.

Trimingham, J. S. 1979. *Christianity among the Arabs in Pre-Islamic Times*. London: Longman.

### The Rape of Lucretia: Sanctity of Body and Soul in Augustine

Adams C. J. and M. M. Fortune (eds) 1995. *Violence against Women and Children: A Chrtistian Theological Sourcebook*. New York: Continuum.

Brown, P. 1988. T*he Body and Society: Men, Women and Sexual Renunciation in Early Christianity*. New York: Columbia University Press.

Burns, J. P. 1984. "Variations on a Dualist Theme: Augustine on the Body and the Soul", in Kopas 1984, 13-26.

Burrus, V. 2013. "Bodies, Desires, Confessions: Shame in Plotinus, Antony and Augustine", in Sère and Wettlaufer 2013, 23-48.

Carney, E. J. 1945. *The Doctrine of St. Augustine on Sanctity*. Washington, DC: The Catholic University of America Press.

Clark, E. A. 1990. "Sex, Shame, and Rhetoric: En-gendering Early Christian Ethics", *Journal of the American Academy of Religion* 59/2: 221-245.

Glendinning, E. 2013. "Reinventing Lucretia: Rape, Suicide and Redemption from Classical Antiquity to the Medieval Era", *International Journal of Classical Tradition* 20: 61-82.

Harper, K. 2013. *From Shame to Sin: The Christian Transformation of Sexual Morality in Late Antiquity*. Cambridge, Massachusetts: Harvard University Press.

Hunter, D. G. 2012. "Augustine on the Body", in Vessey 2012, 353-364.

Kaufman, P. I. 1990. "Augustine, Evil, and Donatism: Sin and Sanctity before the Pelagian Controversy", *Theological Studies* 51: 115-126.

Kopas, J. (ed.) 1984. *Interpreting Tradition: The Art of Theological Reflection*. Chico: Scholars Press, 13-26.

Miles, M. R. 1979. *Augustine on the Body*. Missoula, Montana: Scholars Press.

Miles, M. R. 2012. "From Rape to Resurrection: Sin, Sexual Difference, and Politics", in Wetzel 2012, 75-92.

Muldowney, M. S. *et al.* 1952. Saint Augustine, *Treatises on Various Subjects*. Washington, DC: The Catholic University of America Press.

Pellauer, M. 1995. "Augustine on Rape: On Chapter in the Theological Tradition", in Adams and Fortune 1995, 207-241.

Sato, M. 2015. "The Prohibition of Suicide for Affirmation of Human Beings by Augustine", *Scrinium: Journal of Patrology and Critical Hagiography* 11/1: 135-142.

Sère, B. and J. Wettlaufer (eds) 2013. *Shame Between Penance and Punishment*. Florence: SISMEL-Edizioni del Galluzzo.

Shaw, B. D. 2011. *Sacred Violence: African Christians and Sectarian Hatred in the Age of Augustine*. Cambridge (etc.): Cambridge University Press.

Van der Horst, P. W. 1971. "A Pagan Platonist and a Christian Platonist on Suicide", *Vigiliae Christianae* 25: 282-288.

Vessey, M. (ed.) 2012. *A Companion to Augustine*. West Sussex: Blackwell Publishing.

Von Balz, Horst and Gerhard Schneider (eds) 1992. *Exegetisches Wörterbuch zum Neuen Testament*. Stuttgart; Berlin; Köln: Kohlhammer.

Walsh, P. G. (ed.) 2005. *Augustine, De Civitate Dei Books I & II*. Oxford: Oxbow Books.

Webb, M. 2013. "'On Lucretia who slew herself': Rape and Consolation in Augustine's *De ciuitate dei*", *Augustinian Studies* 44/1: 37-58.

Wetzel, J. (ed.) 2012. *Augustine's* City of God: *A Critical Guide*. Cambridge (etc.): Cambridge University Press.

Wilkinson, K. 2015. *Women and Modesty in Late Antiquity*. Cambridge (etc.): Cambridge University Press.

### A Fluidity of Canon and Textual Criticism in the Works of Origen

#### *Sources*

Aristotle, *Poetica*, in R. Kassel (ed.) 1965. *Aristotelis de arte poetica liber*. Oxford: Clarendon Press 1965.

Aristotle, *Poetics*, transl. W. H. Fyfe 1932. London: Cambridge University Press. (http://www.perseus.tufts.edu/hopper/text?doc=Perseus:text:1999.01.0056).

Eusebius, *Historia ecclesiastica*, in G. Bardy (ed.) 1952-1958. *Eusèbe de Césarée. Histoire ecclésiastique*, 3 vols, Sources chrétiennes 31, 41, 55. Paris: Éditions du Cerf.

Origen, *Commentarium in evangelium Matthaei*, in E. Klostermann (ed.) 1937. *Origenes Werke*, vol. 10.2, Die griechischen christlichen Schriftsteller 40.2. Leipzig: Teubner.

Origen, *Epistula ad Africanum*, in N. de Lange (ed.) 1983. *Origène: Philocalie, 1-20: Sur les écritures, Lettre à Africanus sur l'histoire de Suzanne*, Sources chrétiennes 302. Paris: Edition du Cerf. Transl. A. C. Coxe, J. Donaldson, and A. Roberts (eds) 1885. *Ante-Nicene Fathers IV*. Buffalo, New York: Christian Literature Publishing Co.

Origen, *Commentarii in evangelium Joannis*, in C. Blanc (ed.) 1975. *Origène. Commentaire sur saint Jean*, 3 vols, Sources chrétiennes 222. Paris: Éditions du Cerf. Transl. A. Menzies and J. Donaldson (eds) 1886. *Ante-Nicene Fathers IX*. New York: C. Scribner's Sons; *Commentary on the Gospel according to John: Books I, II, IV, V, VI, X*. R.E. Heine (transl.) 1989. Washington: The Catholic University of America Press.

Origen, *Selecta in Psalmos (fragmenta e catenis)*, in J.-P. Migne (ed.) 1857-1866. *Patrologiae cursus completus (series Graeca)*, MPG 12. Paris: J.P. Migne's Imprimerie Catholique.

Origen, *Philocalia*, in M. Harl (ed.) 1983. *Origène, Philocalie, 1-20 sur les Ecritures*, SC 302. Paris 1983. Transl. G. Lewis 1911. Origen, *The Philocalia of Origen. A Compilation of Selected Passages from Origen's Works Made by St. Gregory of Nazianzus and St. Basil of Caesarea*. Edinburgh: T. & T. Clark. (http://www.tertullian.org/fathers/origen_philocalia_02_text.htm).

Origen, *Contra Celsum*, in M. Borret (ed.) 1967. *Origène. Contre Celse*, vol. 2, Sources chrétiennes 136. Paris: Éditions du Cerf. Transl. A. C. Coxe, J. Donaldson, and A. Roberts (eds) 1885. *Ante-Nicene Fathers IV.* Buffalo, New York: Christian Literature Publishing Co.

Origen, *In Jeremiam Homiliae*, in P. Nautin (ed.) 1976. *Origène. Homélies sur Jérémie*, vol. 2, Sources chrétiennes 238. Paris: Éditions du Cerf.

### Secondary Literature

Adriaanse, H. J. 1998. "Canonicity and the problem of the golden mean," in A. Van der Kooij and K. Van der Toorn (eds), *Canonization and decanonization*, Papers presented to the International Conference of the Leiden Institute for the study of Religions (LISOR) held at Leiden. Leiden: Brill, 313-330.

Barton, J. 2013. "The Old Testament Canons", in J. Carleton Paget and J. Schaper (eds), *The New Cambridge History of the Bible.* Cambridge, New York: Cambridge UP, 389-411.

Becker, E-M. and S. Scholz (eds) 2011. *Kanon in Konstruktion und Dekonstruktion: Kanonisierungsprozesse religiöser Texte von der Antike bis zur Gegenwart.* Berlin, Boston: De Gruyter.

Cerquiglini, B. 1999. *In Praise of the Variant: A Critical History of Philology*, transl. B. Wing. Baltimore: Johns Hopkins UP.

Grafton, A. and M. Williams 2008. *Christianity and the Transformation of the Book: Origen, Eusebius, and the library of Caesarea.* London: Harvard UP.

Kloppenborg, J. S. 2014. "Literate Media in Early Christ Groups: The Creation of a Christian Book Culture", *Journal of Early Christian Studies* 22/1: 21-59.

Larsen, M. 2017. "Accidental Publication, Unfinished Texts and the Traditional Goals of New Testament Textual Criticism", *Journal for the Study of the New Testament* 39/4: 362-387.

Lundhaug, H. and L. I. Lied 2017. "Studying Snapshots: On Manuscript Culture, Textual Fluidity, and New Philology", in L. I. Lied and H. Lundhaug (eds), *Snapshots of Evolving Traditions: Jewish and Christian Manuscript Culture, Textual Fluidity, and New Philology.* Berlin: De Gruyter.

Lundhaug, H. 2008. "Cognitive Poetics and Ancient Texts", in W. Ostreng (ed.), *Complexity. Interdisciplinary Communications 2006/2007.* Centre for Advanced Study, Oslo, 18-22.

Lundhaug, H. 2010. "Canon and Interpretation: A Cognitive Perspective", in E. Thomassen (ed.), *Canon and Canonicity: The Formation and Use of Scripture.* Copenhagen: Museum Tusculanums Forlag, 67-90.

McDonald, L. M. 2002. *Identifying Scripture and Canon in the Early Church: The Criteria Question.* Peabody, MA: Hendrickson.

McDonald, L. M. 2002. "Appendix C: List and Catalogues of Old Testament Collections" and "Appendix D: List and Catalogues of New Testament Collections", in L. M. McDonald and J. M. Sanders (eds), *The Canon Debate.* Peabody, MA: Hendrickson, 585-597.

McDonald, L. M. 1995. *The formation of the Christian Biblical canon.* Peabody, MA: Hendrickson.

McDonald, L. M. and J. M. Sanders (eds). 2002. *The Canon Debate.* Peabody, MA: Hendrickson.

McGuckin, J. A. 2003. "Origen as literary critic in the Alexandrian tradition", in L. Perrone (ed.), *Origeniana Octava: Origen and the Alexandrian Tradition. Leuven: Peeters, 121-135.*

Metzger, B. 1987. *The Canon of the New Testament: Its Origin, Development, and Significance.* Oxford: Clarendon.

Metzger, B. M. 1963. "Explicit References in the Works of Origen to Variant Readings in New Testament Manuscripts", in J. N. Birdsall and R. W. Thomson (eds), *Biblical and Patristic Studies: In Memory of Robert Pierce Casey.* New York: Herder, 78-95.

Nagy, G. 2000. "Review on: Martin L. West (ed.), Homeri Ilias. Recensuit / testimonia congessit. Volumen prius, rhapsodias I–XII continens. Stuttgart and Leipzig: Bibliotheca Teubneriana, 1998. Pp. lxii + 372", *Bryn Mawr Classical Review.* (http://bmcr.brynmawr.edu/2000/2000-09-12.html#n16).

Nienhoff, M. 2011. *Jewish Exegesis and Homeric Scholarship in Alexandria.* Cambridge: Cambridge UP.

Parcer, D. C. 2013. "The New Testament Text and Versions", in J. Carleton Paget and J. Schaper (eds) 2013. *The New Cambridge History of the Bible.* Cambridge: Cambridge UP, 412- 455.

Schneemelcher, W. and Wilson, R.M. (eds), 2003. *New Testament Apocrypha.* Westminster John Knox Press, 2003.

Vos, H.M. 1998. "The canon as a straitjacket", in A. Van der Kooij and K. Van der Toorn (eds), "Canonization and decanonization", *Papers presented to the International Conference of the Leiden Institute for the Study of Religions (LISOR) held at Leiden 9-10 January 1997.* Leiden: Brill, 351-370.

Verheyden, J. 2013. "The New Testament Canon", in J. Carleton Paget and J. Schaper (eds), *The New Cambridge History of the Bible.* Cambridge, New York: Cambridge UP, 389-411.

# INDEX OF NAMES

# INDEX OF SUBJECTS